Date Due

T

30-3

RCMP
The Real Subversives

By
Richard Fidler

Richard Fidler is a staff writer for the newspaper **Socialist Voice**, and a member of the Central Committee of the Revolutionary Workers League. He is the author of **Canada: Accomplice in Apartheid**, **Red Power in Canada: The Native Struggle Today** and **Wage Controls: What They Mean, How to Fight Them**.

Copyright 1978 by Vanguard Publications
All rights reserved
ISBN 0-88758-036-X cloth
ISBN 0-88758-037-8 paper
Printed and bound in Canada 1978

International Distributors:
UNITED STATES: Pathfinder Press Inc., 410 West Street, New York, N.Y. 10014
ENGLAND: Pathfinder Press, 47 The Cut, London, SE1 8LL
AUSTRALIA: Pathfinder Press, 139 St. Johns Road, Glebe 2037, Sydney
NEW ZEALAND: Pilot Books, Box 3398, Wellington

Published in Canada by VANGUARD PUBLICATIONS
Distributed by PATHFINDER PRESS Ltd.,
25 Bulwer Street, Toronto, Ontario M5T 1A1, Canada

Table of Contents

CANADA

DON'T · GET · CAUGHT

ROYAL · CANADIAN·MOUNTED · POLICE

David Poholko/Socialist Voice

1. Canada's Political Police at Work

The cover-up unravels

It all began as if by accident. A junior RCMP officer, Cpl. Robert Samson, on trial in Montreal in March 1976 in connection with a mysterious bombing incident, blurted out that he "had done worse things." Pressed for details, Samson mentioned a 1972 break-in at the offices of the Agence de Presse Libre du Quebec.

A sensational disclosure. The burglary in October 1972 had incapacitated the APLQ, a radical news agency and information source for the Quebec left. The burglars had taken subscribers' lists, bank records, minutes, addressograph plates, and all the administrative and news clippings files, including 200 files on community organizations and unions. Also raided were co-tenants of the building, the Movement for the Defense of Quebec Political Prisoners and a household moving co-op.

Police involvement had been widely suspected at the time. But Quebec provincial police denied any participation; a Montreal police investigation lapsed allegedly for lack of leads; and Ottawa officials failed to answer a registered letter from the APLQ charging RCMP complicity in the raid.

As a result of Samson's revelations, senior officers of the three police forces were brought to trial, in May 1977. But no further details emerged on what had happened. Following secret testimony the cops were given "unconditional discharges," and the judge praised their "noble motives."

The APLQ affair raised some intriguing questions.

● Had the cops been charged with breaking and entering, they could have been compelled to testify publicly about the break-in.

Why were they allowed to plead guilty on a minor charge of failing to obtain a search warrant?

● The cops claimed the APLQ break-in had helped frustrate terrorist plans to carry out kidnappings, hijackings, and assassinations. But no evidence was produced to confirm these claims. No arrests were made, no charges laid.

● Were top federal officials, including the solicitor general, really unaware of the RCMP's involvement, as they claimed? Why was Donald Cobb, the RCMP officer who authorized the break-in, promoted shortly afterward, becoming executive assistant to the deputy solicitor general? And why was Cobb assigned to prepare the official report on the break-in, following Samson's disclosure?

● Federal Solicitor General Francis Fox rejected calls for a public inquiry, insisting the police break-in at the APLQ was an "isolated and exceptional" act. But only months earlier, in January 1977, opposition MPs had revealed the existence of a secret "enemies" blacklist of civil servants circulating among members of the Trudeau cabinet. The list appeared to be compiled from material stolen in December 1970 during a suspicious break-in and fire at the Toronto offices of Praxis Corporation, a research organization helping to organize welfare rights groups. The RCMP, while disclaiming involvement in the theft, admitted it had obtained the stolen material and transmitted it to then Solicitor General Jean-Pierre Goyer.

● Were there other secret blacklists making the rounds? What methods were used to compile them?

In November 1976, RCMP officers had told a Quebec Human Rights Commission inquiry into the firing of radicals at the Olympics that the force kept political files in Ottawa on hundreds of thousands of Canadians suspected of holding dissident views. But the federal solicitor general refused to release information on these files, saying that disclosure would compromise "sources of information, methods of collecting information, the personnel involved in these investigations, as well as the extent and scope of these investigations. . . ."

What was going on?

In the face of mounting public debate over these issues, and the clear evidence of a cover-up by the police, the courts, and the federal government, the newly-elected Parti Quebecois government came under strong pressure to probe further.

The Quebec Justice ministry had initially shown little readiness to press the issue. Its prosecutor agreed to allow the three cops indicted in the APLQ break-in to plead guilty on the lesser charge, and supported defense lawyers' claims that the APLQ break-in was intended to counter "international terrorism." The PQ government failed to appeal the unconditional discharge ruling as it had every right to do. And it failed to lay charges against other police implicated in the break-in.

However, the PQ also sensed an opportunity to embarrass Ottawa, and to build support for its demand that some aspects of RCMP policing in Quebec be turned over to the Quebec government. In mid-June it appointed a one-man commission to investigate the APLQ break-in. The mandate of commissioner Jean Keable was later extended to cover other illegal actions of the RCMP.

The fat was in the fire. Faced with a Quebec inquiry it could not directly control, the Trudeau government needed a smoke-screen. Three weeks after Keable's appointment, Ottawa established its own inquiry, the McDonald commission.

The mandate of each commission was formulated with a view to restricting and controlling disclosures of police activities. The Keable inquiry was limited to specified incidents that the PQ government had an interest in exposing. The McDonald inquiry's mandate was broader, but emphasized that its purpose was to propose means of strengthening "security" procedures and policies. Each inquiry was guaranteed to reflect the views of the government that appointed it: Keable is a Parti Quebecois member; the McDonald commissioners all have well-established Liberal ties.

Disruption . . . 'from time immemorable'

But these precautions could not stem the flow of disclosures of Mountie crimes that began in the summer of 1977. Fearing their heads would roll, individual members of the RCMP security service talked to the press. Yes, they said, they had broken the law, many times, in many ways, but they had only acted under orders from above.

Revelations of these activities began to mushroom October 28, 1977, when Solicitor General Francis Fox told Parliament that the RCMP had staged a break-in in 1973 to steal Parti Quebecois membership lists and financial records. Details on the operation were later revealed in police testimony before the Keable and McDonald commissions.

As each disclosure fed further disclosures, it became clear beyond doubt that Operation Bricole (Odd Job), the police code name for the APLQ burglary, was only one such operation among many.

On November 13, 1977, Fox admitted what was now obvious: "Going through the files, it is very clear that these operations—break-ins and mail diversion and opening—have been going on from almost time immemorable within the force."

The chronology beginning on page 21 reconstructs a partial history of police crimes now revealed to have occurred over the last eight years. It points to the existence of a massive conspiracy against the democratic rights of Canadians and Quebecois, formulated at the top levels of government.

Under exotic code names like Cathedral, Cobra, Vampire, and Puma, an extensive apparatus of police and military forces has carried out surveillance, disruption, and sabotage against opponents, or potential opponents, of government policies. Masterminding the whole campaign has been the RCMP security service. The SS maintains close liaison with provincial and municipal "intelligence" forces; and its central data bank in Ottawa contains copies of political files compiled by other levels of police.

As the chronology indicates, Quebec has been a major arena for these political police activities. Targets include nationalist organizations and parties, unions (especially in the public sector), rank-and-file citizens groups, radical publishing houses and organizations, journalists, student organizations, immigrant rights groups, the women's movement, and civil liberties groups.

Testifying before the Keable inquiry in October 1977 police captain Roger Cormier of the Montreal police antiterrorist squad said his force had no fewer than "250 to 350 movements" under surveillance—using spies, infiltration, wiretaps, and search techniques.

Extensive political policing is carried on in English Canada, too. Reported victims include unions, the New Democratic Party, the National Farmers Union, Native groups, and immigrant and student organizations.

In the case of the NDP, known police tactics have ranged from keeping a file on the personal life of federal NDP leader Ed

Broadbent to conducting an intensive investigation of the Ontario NDP in the early 1970s.

Publicity surrounding these revelations has focused on the various police techniques—the burglaries, break-ins, mail tampering, wiretapping, acts of arson, and frame-up attempts. Some of the most sensational disclosures have concerned the activities of the RCMP's secret "dirty tricks" squads. One such grouping, G-4, described to the Keable inquiry by RCMP Sgt. Claude Brodeur, stole dynamite, carried out break-ins, and even burned down a barn allegedly to prevent a meeting between members of the so-called Quebec Liberation Front (FLQ) and the U.S. Black Panthers.

Other "dirty tricks" include the exploitation of what Brodeur called "character weaknesses" to intimidate activists and in some cases to blackmail them to become informers. An RCMP document dated June 11, 1971, released to the McDonald commission, outlined methods of "disruption, coercion and compromise" to be used for "source development"—that is, the recruitment of informers. These "disruptive tactics," it says, should include "making use of sophisticated and well-researched plans built around existing situations such as power struggles, love affairs, fraudulent use of funds, information on drug abuse, etc. to cause dissension and splintering of the separatist/terrorist groups."

Disruptive tactics can also include outright provocation, designed to get the target group or individuals to commit illegal actions that would expose them to criminal prosecution if not destruction.

Much less attention has been paid to the impact of these police practices on the lives of the victims.

The brief submitted to the McDonald commission by the Revolutionary Workers League, published in this book, documents some of the ways in which revolutionary socialists in English Canada and Quebec have been harassed by the political police. The incidents described are typical of the experiences of many other socialists and political dissidents of widely varying views and affiliations in both nations.

The RWL brief also replies to some of the main arguments the police and their defenders use to justify these practices.

Articles following the brief illustrate techniques used by the political police—from infiltration and provocation of Black,

Native, and immigrant organizations, to inciting right-wing racist thugs to attack radicals and minority ethnic groups.

Behind police crimes—the crisis of the Canadian state

Samson's disclosure of the APLQ break-in may have been accidental. But it is no accident that the RCMP's political role is coming under intense scrutiny at this time. The Canadian ruling class today confronts the worst economic situation since the 1930s, and its most serious political crisis since Confederation. Its response to both challenges entails increased repression, including stepped-up political policing. However, the same conditions also stimulate opposition to government policies and undermine public tolerance of repression.

The 1974-75 international economic slump signalled the definitive end of the postwar capitalist boom. It opened a new period of relative stagnation, in which upturns would be fewer and more shallow, downturns longer and deeper.

Declining profit levels and increasing international competition are driving Canadian capitalists to step up their attacks on workers' incomes, living standards—and democratic rights.

The turn to wage controls in the fall of 1975 was the most dramatic evidence of the shift in ruling-class strategy. Other aspects of the antilabor offensive are the cutbacks in education and social services, anti-union legislation, restrictions on immigration, and attacks on Quebec's attempts to defend the French language.

Controls have appreciably lowered real wage levels. But there has been no marked improvement in Canada's economic standing. All signs point to a continued drive against labor by business and government.

There is the beginning of an important social polarization in Canada. Its first signs were in the struggle against wage controls, which reached its high point with the massive cross-country strike and demonstrations on October 14, 1976. Today labor is beginning to mobilize against the highest unemployment levels since the Great Depression.

The RCMP revelations have indicated the extent of police interest in organized labor. Public sector unions, major targets of the antilabor drive, have been especially singled out for surveillance and disruption. There is every reason to expect more of this activity in the future, as class polarization and the accompanying breakdown of social consensus make it increasingly difficult for the capitalists to rule through "normal," "democratic" means.

The biggest challenge facing Canada's rulers, however, is the Quebec nationalist upsurge and the challenge it poses to the continued existence of the Canadian state. In recent years, and especially since the victory of the Parti Quebecois in November 1976, they have been preoccupied by the prospect that Quebec might leave Confederation. They have no intention of conceding Quebec's right to self-determination.

Quebec is a major component geographically of the Canadian state. It accounts for a quarter of the capitalists' markets within Canada. It has vital mineral resources. Passing through it is the St. Lawrence seaway, providing navigational access to the Atlantic for central and western Canada.

Quebec's oppression is a mainstay of Canadian capitalism. Because francophones suffer discrimination in jobs and income, Quebec is a reservoir of cheap labor, and thus a source of superprofits for Canadian corporations. Anti-Quebec chauvinism, based on that oppression, divides and weakens the labor movement across Canada.

Removal of their direct political control over Quebec would make Canadian capitalists' investments there less secure. Quebec's independence would in fact put a question mark over the economic and political viability of the remaining Canadian state.

The implications were spelled out in a recent article by John Starnes, former director-general of the RCMP security service. Writing in *Survival*, a publication of the International Institute of Strategic Studies, Starnes said "There is no assurance that Canada could survive the shock of dismemberment; death might be inescapable, even if not immediate."

"Canada's internal political situation," Starnes reminded his international audience, "is such that for the first time since NATO was formed, there is now a potential threat to the security of the North American heartland in which are located the principal vital military components of the Alliance."

Washington, of course, shares this assessment. The Pentagon is known to have already prepared studies of the situation in Quebec, and to have rehearsed plans to intervene militarily if necessary. Its first line of defense, however, is the government in Ottawa; and the U.S. Congress was duly appreciative when

Trudeau assured it, in early 1977, that he would never tolerate the break-up of Canada.

Who are the real conspirators?

Increasingly, the operations of the RCMP's security services have been directed toward countering this threat. "As early as 1966," Francis Fox told Parliament recently, "it was recognized by the government that greater attention would have to be given by the security service to ascertaining and assessing the nature and the extent of the separatist threat in Canada, with a view to identifying those individuals, groups and organizations whose real or apparent purpose and objective was to subvert or destroy . . . Canada as a united country under confederation."

Political policing is a major aspect of Ottawa's "national unity" offensive.

The "threat" of a supposed terrorist network, the "Front de Liberation du Quebec" (FLQ), has been skilfully used to portray the entire independentist movement in Quebec as an undemocratic conspiracy, to minimize the movement's popular support, and to justify the use of repressive measures against it. The police stole Parti Quebecois files, we are told, because they suspected the PQ had been "infiltrated" by the FLQ.

Yet we now know that the authorities had so much difficulty finding any evidence of FLQ terrorism and threats that they often had to fabricate it themselves.

An accurate and authoritative estimate of the "FLQ" was presented by Pierre Vallieres in *L'Urgence de Choisir*. the book that described his renunciation of the terrorist strategy. Vallieres, who was often described in the mass media as the FLQ's "theoretician," said "there has never been an FLQ organization as such, but only cells or small groups limited in number, in strength, and in means, without organic links, without central direction, and without a true strategy." (*L'Urgence de Choisir*, Editions Parti-Pris, 1971, p. 137)

Tiny groups like the FLQ that incorrectly seek to substitute the armed actions of a few for the action of the masses are particularly vulnerable to manipulation by the state's repressive agencies. Vallieres noted this himself, in a passage worth recalling: "...as I have emphasized several times, the letters 'FLQ' can be made use of by any agent provocateur in the pay of the RCMP or the CIA, without the danger of this agent being identified or denounced by anyone answerable to an organization with leadership, direction, or means of control." (*Ibid.*, p. 138)

It is precisely because the ruling class confronts a *mass* movement, and not a tiny group of would-be conspirators isolated from the masses, that it has had to create an immense arsenal of repressive agencies and techniques.

The real conspiracy is the federalist campaign against Quebec, orchestrated by the Trudeau government. It encompasses a combination of repressive tactics.

Economic blackmail. Big business and government issue repeated warnings of economic sabotage if Quebec separates—threats underscored by highly publicized evidence of the beginning of a "flight of capital," such as the Sun Life exodus. Ontario's Conservative premier William Davis has rejected outright the PQ's proposals for economic association between a "sovereign" Quebec and Ontario.

Political blackmail. Threats by Ottawa to disallow Quebec legislation; initiation of a purge of "separatists" at Radio-Canada; constitutional confrontations with Quebec. Francophones throughout Canada have been blackmailed with federal promises of a trade-off of language rights for French-speaking minorities outside Quebec in return for concessions to the privileged English-speaking minority in Quebec.

Ottawa has openly encouraged Quebec anglophones to defy the Quebec government's language law, hoping to use this opposition to create a powerful striking force of non-francophones against the independentists and their allies. Federalist forces in Quebec are being regrouped and reinforced, in particular through the rebuilding of the Liberal party.

In English Canada, Ottawa is working actively to forge a monolith of chauvinist opposition to Quebec's rights.

And looming not very far in the background is the threat to use armed force. Trudeau trotted it out again in a year-end 1977 interview with CTV, and in doing so demonstrated the undemocratic essence of the federalist offensive.

There is no legal way Quebec can become independent, said the prime minister. And if Quebec attempts something illegal, "I'm not going to be shy about using the sword," he said, driving the point home with a reference to his use of the War Measures Act in 1970.

Trudeau's concern for "legality" is touching, especially in light of his repeated defense of illegality by the federal police. Nevertheless, his position that the creation of an independent Quebec—even following a democratic decision by the majority of Quebecois—is illegal, contains a useful lesson on the relation between legality and democracy. They are by no means always the same, and in fact are sometimes counterposed. We have it on the authority of the prime minister.

'Rule of law'—guarantor of democratic rights?

Alarmed that revelations of police crimes—and the government's defense of them—are undermining the credibility of capitalist law and justice, many liberal critics of the government call for a reassertion of "the rule of law." Arbitrary practices, they imply, are limited to departures from the law. Adherence to lawful procedures will guarantee the protection of everyone's democratic rights.

This is wrong on two counts.

First, in a capitalist democracy formal equality of all citizens before the law is vitiated in practice by their underlying social inequality. As Anatole France put it, a rich capitalist has as much right to sleep under a bridge as a beggar.

Secondly, the law itself is an expression of the underlying social and political relationship of forces. Capitalist laws, the ground rules of a system based on private property and privilege, enforce and reproduce inequality and injustice. And that is the role of all the state institutions that collectively make up "the rule of law"—the legislature that formulates the laws, the courts that interpret and apply them, and the police and prisons that enforce them. Because capitalist rule is arbitrary and unjust, the "rule of law" is too.

This is nowhere more evident than in the realm of "national security," the pretext for the RCMP's crimes. Laws and practices aimed at the protection of the state reduce capitalist rule to its simplest, most arbitrary elements. The crudest expressions occur in time of war. During the last world war, for example, Japanese Canadians were uprooted from their homes and interned in concentration camps, their property was confiscated and sold by the government. Jehovah's Witnesses and pacifist groups were outlawed, along with revolutionary socialist organizations. Opponents of conscription were jailed in Quebec, even though the Quebecois had voted by more than 80 percent against conscription. All of this was thoroughly undemocratic—and completely "legal."

Such practices are by no means limited to times of war, however. In fact, the notion of "national security" first received legal expression in the wake of the 1919 Winnipeg General Strike, through changes in the Criminal Code and the immigration law. For years Marxist organizations were effectively outlawed under Section 98 of the Criminal Code. Significantly, when the Trudeau government brought in its draft Public Order Act under the War Measures in 1970, the wording was modelled closely on the old Section 98.

The War Measures Act itself was in force for no less than 40 percent of the time between the First World War and 1970; emergency powers implemented under the act during the Second World War were not suspended until 1954.

Governments in Canada have become accustomed to employing harsh laws to repress political dissent. According to a Quebec study, Canada has had more prosecutions for sedition in the last 70 years than England had in 400 years. (*Terrorisme et Justice*, by Jean-Louis Baudoin, Jacques Fortin, and Denis Szabo; Editions du Jour, 1970) Some recent examples were the prosecutions of Raymond Lemieux, the leader of the struggle for a unilingual French school system in Quebec, in 1969; and of Montreal labor leader Michel Chartrand in 1969 and 1970. It is not always necessary to convict under such laws; the expense and hardship endured by defendants is sufficient to deter others.

The use of repression as an instrument of government policy is rooted in the very nature of Canada. Like the Czarist empire, the Canadian state is a veritable "prison house of nations." It was built on the oppression of the Quebecois, the near-annihilation of Native peoples, and the degradation of the Acadiens and other francophones outside Quebec. These peoples, comprising more than one third of the present population of Canada, were never asked if they assented to Confederation. And the Quebecois are not the only ones today to be questioning the value of remaining in Canada. Moreover, extreme differences of wealth and privilege within Canadian society as a whole have created a history of deepgoing class struggles. Holding such a state together has required more than a little coercion, both legal and extralegal.

Making legal what's illegal

It is futile to look to the institutions of capitalist rule—the laws, parliament, the courts—to guarantee democratic rights. The capitalists have no hesitation in trampling on these rights, and their own "legality," at the least sign that their interests are in jeopardy.

That's why Trudeau shows little embarrassment at the fact that some police activities violate the formal provisions of the law. If the actions are illegal, he says, we'll make them legal.

And that's just what the government has been doing in recent years. The War Measures crisis marked a turning point in this respect.

Shortly after the Public Order Act was introduced, Parliament amended the Federal Court Act to permit a minister, on production of an affidavit, to prevent access by a court to any document whose disclosure would in the minister's opinion be prejudicial to "national security" . . . and (among other things) "federal-provincial relations." Ottawa has used the law to stymie the operations of the Keable commission, and before that, to obstruct the Quebec Human Rights Commission investigation into the Olympics firings.

This was followed in 1974 with the legalization of wiretapping; in 1977, police wiretap powers were extended even further.

In 1976 the Citizenship Act was amended to authorize the federal cabinet to refuse citizenship on national security grounds without having to divulge the reasons. And in August 1977 the new Immigration Act, Law C-24, was adopted, greatly restricting entry to Canada and permanent residence status on grounds of "national security."

The Trudeau government is now rushing through Parliament a bill to legalize what the police admit they have been doing illegally for more than 40 years: opening first-class mail. The bill, modelled on the earlier wiretap legislation, would permit any police force to open mail on the sole authorization of the solicitor general, if they claim "national security" is at stake. The purpose of the bill is not to stop crimes, as the RCMP and government allege, but to give the Mounties further immunity from prosecution in their harassment of political opponents of the government.

Examining the pattern of legislation, the Quebec-based Human

Rights League was led to conclude in a recent study that "the federal government is introducing 'war measures' piece by piece, by providing each of its principal pieces of legislation with exceptional or extraordinary powers."

The McDonald commission is also part of this strategy. Its mandate, as outlined by Francis Fox, is "to help us . . . in our search for ways to improve the working of the security service in the vital role assigned to it for the protection of our national security." (House of Commons, July 6, 1977)

All these changes in the law, of course, merely reflect the increased reliance of Canadian capitalism on permanent repression as a means of rule. While social services are being cut back and wages restricted, spending on the police and military is rising to unprecedented "peacetime" levels. The 1978-79 federal budget projects an increase in armed forces expenditures by almost $400 million. Most of that amount will be used to purchase new tanks and armored cars designed for "civil insurrections." Public sector staff levels have been frozen, but military, RCMP, and prison personnel will increase. Over the next four years Ottawa will build ten new penitentiaries in Quebec, although Quebec is the only province in Canada where the crime rate has *decreased* in the last 15 years.

Political policing and the fight for democratic rights

RCMP "dirty tricks" are a fundamental aspect of the developing capitalist offensive against the working class and the Quebec nationalist movement. Their exposure helps to weaken that offensive. The revelations of illegal activities serve to undermine the image of a democratic Canada; they strengthen nationalist sentiment in Quebec and discredit propaganda for "national unity" at the expense of workers' living standards and democratic rights. Moreover, the disclosures of RCMP political witch-hunting weaken the effectiveness of the RCMP as a major instrument of federalist oppression in Quebec.

The fight against RCMP crimes is an integral part of the defense of Quebec's right to self-determination. And it is an example of how the defense of Quebec is in the interests of English-Canadian workers. If Ottawa can get away with repressing the Quebec nationalist movement, it will be reinforced in its attacks on the English-Canadian working class.

Likewise, the struggle to expose and combat RCMP crimes

against the workers movement strengthens the leading edge of the nationalist struggle in Quebec, and in English Canada aids in the defense of the major potential ally of the Quebecois in their struggle against the Canadian state.

Where mass sentiment is mobilized in opposition to repression, it is possible to deal powerful blows against the government witch-hunters and their reactionary laws. Opposition to the Quebec sedition trials following the War Measures crisis resulted in the dropping of charges against most defendants, and acquittals of others. The federal government prosecuted Dr. Henry Morgentaler three times for performing illegal abortions; three times Quebec juries refused to convict him, reflecting overwhelming public opposition to Canada's restrictive abortion laws.

Unfortunately, since the revelations of RCMP crimes began to unfold, there has been no centralized response by the victims. The trade unions, the NDP leadership, and most civil liberties groups have defaulted in their responsibilities.

The Canadian Labor Congress leadership, in a brief submitted to the McDonald commission, actually *endorsed* police surveillance and harassment of the labor movement. It suggested that police intervention in the unions was justified in order to root out "communist" and "separatist" influence. The CLC, it said, "recognizes a need for national security." It worried only that the RCMP's antisubversive activity would be misused by "overzealous people," that is, directed against what the brief called "legitimate" union activities.

The CLC and most of its affiliated unions have said very little about revelations that the RCMP has spied extensively on many unions. (Notable exceptions are the Canadian Union of Public Employees and the Canadian Union of Postal Workers, which have issued strong denunciations of police activities in the labor movement.)

The New Democratic Party leadership have also failed to mount an effective protest against RCMP crimes, including evidence of RCMP intervention in the party. British Columbia NDP leader Dave Barrett scoffed at reports, subsequently confirmed, that his cabinet had been spied on by the Mounties. In Ontario, NDP leader Stephen Lewis failed to protest when the province's attorney general confirmed reports of RCMP surveillance of the party. Federal leader Ed Broadbent showed some diligence in attempting (unsuccessfully) to get access to his own RCMP file. But

Broadbent and the rest of the NDP parliamentary caucus, alarmed that the RCMP revelations are undermining a pillar of the Canadian state apparatus, have hesitated to press the issue. Increasingly they have emphasized their fundamental support of the RCMP.

The CLC and NDP leaderships alike accept the underlying rationale for police spying on political dissent. They accept that the capitalist state has a "right" to take coercive measures against those who hold—or are alleged to hold—views that in some way challenge the private property system or the established state structures upholding that system.

Many of these "leaders" have played their own part in reactionary police practices. Some CLC leaders, for example, rose to the offices they hold today during the Cold War witchhunt against Communists and radicals in the labor movement. Union bureaucrats didn't hesitate to enlist the direct aid of the government and its police in their fight against "reds." These purges seriously weakened the labor movement—just as the failure to condemn police intervention today undermines labor's unity.

The membership of the unions and the NDP face a major challenge to reverse these reactionary stances by their leaders. They must strive to build a broad united defense of all the victims of political policing, in both English Canada and Quebec—a powerful movement that can frustrate the government's attempts to increase repressive legislation and strengthen the police.

In Quebec, the Human Rights League has taken a positive initiative with the launching of Operation Liberte—Operation Freedom—a campaign to unite unions, citizens groups, radical organizations, and all the other victims of "national security" policing in a common front. The campaign's first project is to mobilize opposition to the federal bill to legalize police mail tampering.

The Quebec initiative is to be welcomed. It must be carried forward and emulated in English Canada.

It is hoped that this modest book can help stimulate such efforts.

March 28, 1978

Police Operations-A Glossary

Operation Cathedral. Code-name used by the RCMP for the illegal opening of mail, which it has practiced for at least 40 years.

Operation Puma (formerly Operation 300). Break-ins to photograph or photocopy documents and files on the spot. Does not normally include theft of documents.

Operation Cobra. Interception of telephone conversations by wiretap.

Operation Vampire. Interception of conversations using listening devices installed in walls or ceilings.

Technical Source. An electronic listening device, as used in Operations Cobra or Vampire.

Human Source. Information gathering through informers, using infiltration and direct observation techniques.

Operation Odd Job (in French, "Bricole"). Code-name given to the break-in and burglary at the offices of the Agence de Presse Libre and the Quebec Political Prisoners Defense Movement (MDPPQ) on the night of October 6-7, 1972.

Operation Ham. Code-name given to the break-in to steal and copy the membership list of the Parti Quebecois, during the night of January 8-9, 1973.

Operation Duhaime. Code-name given to the installation of an electronic listening dvice in the offices of the Saint-Maurice PQ, in Shawinigan, beginning June 29, 1969.

Operation Ronald. Code-name given by the RCMP to operations aimed at "controlling" alleged FLQ cells in 1972, in particular a cell implicated in a planned aircraft hijacking during the October 1972 federal election campaign.

Operation Quebec-95. An operation launched by the Surete du Quebec (Provincial Police) in early 1973 directed against "movements with national influence in Quebec," making particular use of electronic wiretapping.

Featherbed file. A special RCMP file on prominent personalities in public and private life—politicians, civil servants, journalists, etc.

Disruptive tactics. "Destabilization" tactics, such as harassment and sabotage, used by the RCMP against a given group and even within the group.

2. A Short Chronology of Political Policing

The following chronology of political police operations in Quebec and English Canada has been translated from Operation Liberte, *a pamphlet published in February 1978 by the Quebec Ligue des Droits de l'Homme (Human Rights League). It has been slightly abridged and edited for publication here.*

All the incidents listed have been reported in the news media, or revealed in testimony before the Keable and McDonald inquiries.

The Human Rights League emphasizes that this chronology, which goes back only to 1969, the year before the October Crisis, is "just a first and very partial listing.

"We want to complete it, in so far as possible, with the aid of individuals and groups that have been victims of the political police," it says.

Reprinted with the permission of the Ligue des Droits de l'Homme, 3836 rue Saint-Hubert, Montreal.

Translation copyright Vanguard Publications 1978.

1969

March

● Two plainclothes cops are spotted at the Vieux-Montreal CEGEP (junior college) during a planning meeting for Operation McGill Francais. Hidden in a film projection room, the police are furnished with all the audio-visual material required for political espionage.

June

• On June 29 the Quebec Surete (SQ—provincial police) installs a radio transmitter microphone in the local headquarters of the Saint-Maurice Parti Quebecois association in Shawinigan. "Operation Duhaime" is a joint operation with the RCMP. The listening device is still in place during the Quebec election in April 1970.

• Publication of the report of the federal Royal Commission on Security in Canada. The report, which had been submitted to the government on September 23, 1968, states that the two main threats to "national security" in Canada are "international communism" and "the Quebec separatist movement."

October

• The Canadian Army occupies Montreal during the October 7 strike by municipal police. At a demonstration in front of the offices of the Murray Hill bus company a plainclothes cop mixing with the demonstrators, Cpl. Robert Dumas of the SQ, is killed by a carbine bullet shot by a Murray Hill security agent.

• Beginning October 10, the Montreal police security service, aided by the RCMP, carries out about 30 raids and several arrests aimed primarily at local citizens' committees and the Company of Young Canadians. The warrants, some of them open writs of assistance, refer to Section 60 of the Criminal Code, which deals with sedition.

• On October 11, the chairman of the Montreal executive committee, Lucien Saulnier—Mayor Drapeau's right-hand man—denounces "a plan to overthrow the government" and calls for a royal commission of inquiry into "clearly subversive activities" of "social agitators" in the Company of Young Canadians.

November

• On November 8, the Drapeau-Saulnier administration issues a draft bylaw banning public meetings and demonstrations. This bylaw is adopted November 12 by the city council. [It has recently been upheld by the Supreme Court of Canada.]

• On November 11 two plainclothes cops of the SQ record the words of Michel Chartrand, president of the Montreal Central Council of the Confederation of National Trade Unions (CSN), during a meeting of the CSN's Montreal Construction Union. Chartrand, soon afterwards accused of sedition, was later charged with contempt of court.

• The RCMP investigates the CBC's French news room in Montreal and the CSN Journalists Union. The union president, Michel Bourdon, is later fired.

Autumn 1969

• The RCMP launches an extensive investigation, which is to last three years, into the New Democratic Party (NDP). Using infiltration and electronic surveillance, it compiles files on MPs, leaders, and activists in the party as well as on its finances and its strategy. The RCMP later said it was especially interested in the NDP left-wing, the Waffle group, which was founded in September 1969. It also said it was interested in Trotskyist and "communist" members of the Waffle. The Waffle was dissolved several years later.

1970

February

• On February 25 at the Hotel Nelson in Montreal, the police tape a news conference given by Charles Gagnon (who has just come out of prison after more than three years), Robert Lemieux, and Jacques Larue-Langlois, president of the Comite d'aide au groupe Vallieres-Gagnon.

May

• On May 7, one week after the Quebec elections in which the PQ got 23 percent of the vote, the federal cabinet forms a special committee assigned to consider "measures and procedures to be taken" in the event that the War Measures Act is proclaimed. The committee is also assigned to find ways to strengthen the role of the Army and the RCMP in "maintaining public order."

June

● Police surveillance of the Front d'Action Politique (FRAP), the trade-union-sponsored municipal party that has just been founded in Montreal, and of its neighborhood Political Action Committees (CAPs).

August

● Two police agents provocateurs uncovered by the CSN construction union during the general strike in the building trades.

October

● Proclamation of the War Measures Act and suppression of democratic rights. 500 arrests, 3,000 raids.
● Operation "Essai" of the Canadian Army in Quebec. Groups targeted: unions, PQ, NDP, FRAP, citizens committees, and radical groups.

December

● Charges of sedition laid against the "Five": Michel Chartrand, Robert Lemieux, Jacques Larue-Langlois, Pierre Vallieres and Charles Gagnon. All are later acquitted.
● A police wiretap records a meeting between Robert Lemieux and his client Paul Rose at the Parthenais detention center, in the office of Insp. Denis Viau of the SQ.
● Break-in at offices of Praxis Institute in Toronto. Theft of documents, and fire.
● An amendment to the Federal Court Act allows a minister, by simply producing an affidavit, to prevent a court from divulging a document that might violate "national security" and/or "federal-provincial relations."

1971
April
● On April 10, a microphone is discovered at Repentigny in the

home of Jean-Marie Cossette, local president of the Societe
Nationale des Quebecois (SNQ) and a well known independentist.

● Numerous raids, seizures, and arrests directed against the
Communist Party of Canada (Marxist-Leninist), a Maoist grouping founded in August 1970, and closure by the police of most of
its bookstores.

● Numerous raids directed against the Ligue Socialiste
Ouvriere (LSO), a Trotskyist organization founded in 1964.
Searches, arrests, and compiling of files. [See RWL brief to the
McDonald commission published elsewhere in this book.]

May

● On May 15 a hidden microphone is found in a Montreal
school during the first convention of the Quebec Political
Prisoners Defense Movement (MDPPQ).

● On May 17 Solicitor General Jean-Pierre Goyer authorizes a
telephone wiretap operation against the APLQ (Operation Cobra).
The operation lasted at least until November 1972.

June

● Break-in at the offices of James Lewis & Samuel, Publishers,
in Toronto (today James Lorimer and Co.), which had published
An Unauthorized History of the RCMP.

● The RCMP presents Solicitor General Goyer with a blacklist
of top federal civil servants whom the police describe as "the ex-
traparliamentary opposition."

Summer

● The federal government orders a report on "crisis
management" from Gen. Michael Dare. During the October Crisis
of October 1970 the general had led Operation Essai of the
Canadian Army in Quebec.

● Police surveillance and infiltration at the Petit Quebec Libre
farm at Sainte-Anne-de-la-Rochelle, in the Eastern Townships.

August

● On August 20, break-in at the headquarters of the League for
Socialist Action in Toronto. Theft of membership lists and
numerous documents.

September

• On September 1, establishment of the Security Planning and Analysis Group, reporting directly to Solicitor General Jean-Pierre Goyer in Ottawa. This was the Bourne group, after its director general, Col. Robin Bourne.

• Around the same time, the establishment in utmost secrecy of the Centre d'Analyse et de Documentation (CAD—Analysis and Documentation Center) in Quebec City, like the Bourne group but reporting directly to the office of Premier Robert Bourassa.

October

• On October 29, several agents provocateurs of the Montreal police are spotted during the big union demonstration against *La Presse*, the Montreal daily. A police charge on the demonstration results in one death and dozens of injured.

December

• On December 19, the RCMP issues a fake communique in the name of the "Minerve" cell of the FLQ, denouncing Pierre Vallieres' abandonment of terrorism and his newfound support for the Parti Quebecois.

1972
Spring

• At an undisclosed date the RCMP steals dynamite from a construction site on the South Shore at Montreal (in the Saint-Gregoire-Marieville region). On the following October 23, a week before the federal election, the dynamite is left along Highway 50, about 10 miles from Coaticook. The SQ is advised through an "anonymous call" (from the RCMP) of the location of the dynamite and of its possible possession by a terrorist group.

April

• Utilizing the drug laws, the RCMP raids a cottage at Parent, in the Laurentians, that serves as a meeting place for activists in the APLQ.

• Following a bomb explosion of unknown origin the Montreal police security services search the offices of the Cuban trade delegation in the city—after throwing the Cubans out. This violation of diplomatic immunity is denounced by Havana.

• On April 18-19, the Canadian Army carries out Exercise Neat Pitch: 46 generals and colonels meet to study a plan for possible occupation of Quebec in the event of "apprehended insurrection."

May

• Police infiltration of the interunion Common Front of the 200,000 public-sector workers in Quebec, during the general strike. Since 1971 documents of the Common Front relating to its negotiating stance have been pinched by police and transmitted to the Bourassa government.

• Operation Dragon 1 of the SQ against the Common Front, officially to "forestall action by certain radical and marginal elements" within the unions.

• On May 8 the RCMP burns a barn on the Petit Quebec Libre farm at Sainte-Anne-de-la-Rochelle, in the Eastern Townships, to prevent a meeting that is allegedly to be held there.

• Operation Vampire, the wiretapping of the APLQ and MD-PPQ offices at 3459 rue Saint-Hubert in Montreal, is already under way.

June

• On June 7, Andre Chamard, a lawyer then articling in a radical lawyers' "Commune," is "kidnapped" in a car by two RCMP agents, taken to a secluded place near Saint-Hyacinthe, then bullied and molested to induce him to become an informer.

• A report on the CSN by the Canadian Army information services is dated June 20. The PQ, which unveils this report on September 18, discloses another shortly afterwards on the Confederation of Democratic Trade Unions (CSD). These reports suggest that the main beneficiary of political action by the Quebec unions will be the PQ.

• Police surveillance—and apparently wiretapping—at the Librairie Progressiste [a Maoist bookstore] in Montreal.

October

• During the night of October 6-7, the RCMP, the SQ, and the

Montreal police conduct "Operation Bricole"—Operation Odd Job—a break-in at the offices of the APLQ, the MDPPQ, and the First of May Moving Cooperative. Lists of members and subscribers are stolen, as well as more than 1,000 dossiers (15 file drawers) and addressograph plates belonging to the APLQ. The operation, which had been preceded by "rehearsals," is aimed at dismantling the three organizations. On October 25, another break-in occurs at the home of an APLQ journalist, Louise Vandelac. Three other activists in the agency are also called in for questioning by the police.

• The RCMP is implicated in a plan to hijack an aircraft during the federal election campaign (Operation Ronald). The RCMP now says that since the preceding August it controlled the "FLQ cell" involved in this plan.

December

• On December 3, a break-in at the NDP headquarters in Ottawa. [In the federal election a month earlier, the NDP had taken 30 seats, giving it the "balance of power" in the House of Commons.]
• The RCMP infiltrates the office of the cabinet of Premier Dave Barrett of the NDP in British Columbia. Barrett had been elected in August 1972.

1973

January

• On the night of January 8-9, the RCMP carries out Operation Ham against the Parti Quebecois—a clandestine search under Operation Puma of the offices of Messageries Dynamiques at 9280 rue Jeanne Mance in Montreal. Computer tapes containing membership lists and financial and other confidential information of the PQ are taken and transcribed. The tapes are returned five hours later.
• The Quebec Surete launches Operation Quebec-95, a vast investigation of what the police call "movements with national influence" in Quebec. About a hundred groups are targeted;

political dossiers are compiled on them. The operation makes extensive use of wiretapping.

February

● On February 21, the Montreal police search the Centre des Femmes (Women's Center) in Montreal. Lists and documents are seized on the pretext that they violate the Criminal Code restrictions on abortion.

April

● Wiretaps are installed on the telephones of Yvon Groulx and Gilles Caron, two leaders of the Saint John the Baptist Society (SSJB) in Montreal, under the SQ's Operation Quebec-95. The taps last at least six months.
● Burglary of the offices of the Political Information Committee of the Quebec Film Distribution Council and the General Theatre Union of the CSN.
● Burglary at the offices of *Quebec-Presse*, the trade-union sponsored weekly newspaper in Montreal.

August

● Hidden microphones are discovered in the offices of the APLQ at 3459 rue Saint-Hubert.

September

● Hidden microphones are discovered in the offices of the newspaper *En Lutte* at 3939 rue Saint-Denis in Montreal. The first issue of the paper had just been published on September 13.

October

● The Montreal police conduct a search without warrant at offices rented by the Montreal Central Council of the CSN, at 1015 est, rue Sainte-Catherine.

November

● On November 21, five microphones are discovered in the new offices of the APLQ, at 2074 rue Beaudry. The building, which serves as a meeting place for citizens groups, also houses the First of May Moving Coop and an office for students of the University of Quebec in Montreal. The latter office had been burglarized on October 12.

1974

February

• During the United Aircraft strike in Longueuil, SQ agents contact about a dozen strikers, members of the United Auto Workers (FTQ), and invite them to become informers. Quebec Justice Minister Jerome Choquette tells the National Assembly that this type of operation is "common" in labor conflicts.

• Beginning of the SQ's Operation Raymond—wiretapping ostensibly directed against corrupt unions in the construction industry.

March

• On March 15 the federal government tables the Dare report on "crisis management" in Parliament. At the same time it announces establishment of an "Emergency Measures Planning Center," whose responsibilities include the maintenance of public order in times of crisis.

June

• On June 30 Law C-176, the Protection of Privacy Act, which legalizes wiretapping through amendments to the Official Secrets Act, comes into effect.

July

• On July 26 an RCMP agent, Robert Samson, is wounded in the explosion of a bomb he was placing near the home of a Steinberg executive in Ville Mont-Royal. A conflict is under way between the food chain and a union affiliated to the Quebec Federation of Labor (FTQ).

November

• An RCMP agent Rene Bouliane, alias Jean Gagnon, is hired to work in the kitchens of the Notre-Dame Hospital in Montreal. He later becomes a shop steward for the CSN.

1975

February

• On February 18 four microphones are discovered in offices rented by the Montreal Central Council of the CSN, at 1015 est, rue Sainte-Catherine. These offices have been used since 1971 by unions, citizens and radical groups, and political organizations like the PQ, the FRAP, and the NDP, as well as cooperatives and groups like the Quebec-Palestine Association. Later it is learned that some cops were occupying an office on the first floor of the building opposite.

March

• On March 27 the federal cabinet issues (secret) directives aimed at "clarifying the mandate" of the RCMP Security Service. These directives effectively widen the force's antisubversive mandate, even though Prime Minister Trudeau states that they brought about an end to surveillance of political parties like the PQ and the NDP.
• The CSN identifies an RCMP informer, Pierre Breton, who has been a very active militant in Quebec City since 1966 in several unions and in the provincial political action committee of the CSN.

April

• On April 30 two agents of the RCMP and Montreal police try to recruit the executive secretary of the Montreal CSN central council, Lise Fontaine, as an informer.

May

• RCMP agent Rene Bouliane is a delegate of the Notre Dame

Hospital workers union to the annual convention of the Montreal CSN Central Council.

● On May 20 a full-time employee of the Montreal CSN Central Council, Clermont Bergeron, receives an intimidating visit at his home from two agents of the RCMP and Montreal police.

● Convention of the Canadian Union of Public Employees (CUPE) at Ottawa. The RCMP is involved in a plan to prevent the election of Grace Hartman as president of the union.

● The federal minister of immigration issues (secret) directives urging rejection of immigrants who constitute a "risk to national security."

● The RCMP spies on the activities of immigrant activists and the ‿uebec-Chile Solidarity Committee in Montreal.

June

● On June 25, Montreal police search the offices of the Committee for Contraception and Abortion on Demand and the Feminist Documentation Center in Montreal. Lists and documents are seized on the pretext that they violate the provisions of the Criminal Code.

September

● RCMP agent Rene Bouliane is hired as a file clerk at the Sainte-Justine Hospital in Montreal, where he becomes a member of the CSN union.

November

● On November 21 RCMP agent Jean Desrosiers presents himself as a journalist of the Canadian Press—together with a photographer—during an interview with a strike leader at the E.B. Eddy plant in Hull. The strikers are members of the Canadian Paperworkers Union (FTQ).

December

● The RCMP interrogates Jean-Pierre Bergeron, a full-time employee of the Association cooperative d'economie familiale (Household Economy Cooperative Association—ACEF) in the

Ottawa region, as part of an investigation of local citizens groups, unions, and radical organizations. As part of the same investigation it also interrogates a federal civil servant living in Hull.

● Burglary at the offices of the Quebec City CSN Central Council, in the CSN headquarters at 155 boul. Charest, Quebec City.

1976

February

● Break-ins—twice—at 1212 rue Panet, Montreal, which contains the offices of five organizations: the Professional Federation of Quebec Journalists; the Federation of Household Economy Cooperative Associations of Quebec; the ACEF's Montreal section; the Institute to Promote Consumers' Interests; and the Cooperative Social Policy Research Center.

March

● On March 3 RCMP agent Rene Bouliane is identified by the CSN during a mass meeting of the public sector unions in the Common Front, at the Paul Sauve Center in Montreal.

● With the formation of the second public-sector union Common Front and the strikes accompanying it, the SQ relaunches Operation Dragon (Part 2).

● During his trial for having planted a bomb at the Steinberg executive's home, Robert Samson, now a former RCMP agent, reveals Operation Odd Job against the APLQ—"a movement," he says, "that always had fairly extensive lists of the whole Quebec left."

Spring

● In anticipation of the Olympic Games to be held in July and August in Montreal, the security services of the Canadian Army, the RCMP, the SQ, and the Montreal police launch a vast "cleanup" operation, involving raids, interrogations, and so on, aimed at dozens of militants.

May

• On May 27 the federal cabinet issues (secret) directives with respect to employment and promotion of federal civil servants considered to hold "separatist" views. It is later learned that blacklists were transmitted by the RCMP to the Security Planning and Analysis Group (the Bourne group) and from there to the federal cabinet.

• During the Olympic Games some militants are forced to vacate Montreal and are placed under surveillance.

• Some employees of the Olympic Games Organizing Committee (COJO) or firms linked to COJO are fired for reasons of "national security," without being able to learn why. The police later confirm that at least 20 and possibly 150 persons suffered this fate. [See the case of Katie Curtin, reported in the RWL brief to the McDonald commission.]

• Harassment of activists in the Arab, Haitian, and Chilean ethnic communities, among others.

• The new Canadian Citizenship Law facilitates rejection of citizenship for reasons of "national security."

November

• At least four Quebec leaders of the Canadian Union of Postal Workers (CUPW) are approached by RCMP agents who interrogate them on the internal functioning of the union and on the presence of "leftist" activists in it. The RCMP proposes to Jacques Turmel, vice-president of CUPW's Montreal section, that he become a police "contact."

1977

June

• On June 16 the Quebec government appoints the Keable Commission of Inquiry, with instructions to clear up what happened in the burglary at the APLQ. The commission's mandate was later widened to cover "some police operations in Quebec territory."

July

• On July 6 the federal government announces the creation of

the McDonald Commission of Inquiry into illegal activities of the RCMP and the question of "national security" in Canada.
• The federal wiretap law is amended, becoming more repressive.
• During the night of July 22-23 there is a fire of criminal origin in the offices of the Hochelaga-Maisonneuve neighborhood ACEF, the Household Education Service, and the Community Action Cooperative, on Ontario Street in Montreal.

August

• Parliament adopts the new immigration law C-24, with "national security" restrictions that make it more repressive than preceding legislation.

November

• It is learned that the RCMP has stolen and used medical files and income tax records.
• The Canadian defense minister admits that the security services of the Army and the RCMP installed microphones in student meeting rooms at universities in Toronto, Ottawa, Montreal, and elsewhere, for a period of several years.
• It is learned that for more than 40 years the RCMP has been illegally opening mail (Operation Cathedral).

December

• The Quebec minister of justice, Marc-Andre Bedard, announces that in 1978 the government will establish an "Analysis Group on the Security of the Quebec State," which would be somewhat the equivalent of the Bourne Group in Ottawa. The Quebec body would replace the Centre d'Analyse et de Documentation (CAD), dissolved by the Levesque government. However, it will not report directly to the office of the premier (as the CAD did), but to the Ministry of Justice—more precisely, the deputy minister in charge of public security, Paul Benoit, who is the former director of the Quebec Surete.

3. RCMP: The Real Subversives

The following is the text of the brief submitted to the federal government's McDonald commission by the Revolutionary Workers League. It was presented at a public hearing of the commission in Toronto January 18, 1978 by a delegation of the RWL led by Richard Fidler and Bret Smiley.

Introduction

We welcome this opportunity to present the views of the Revolutionary Workers League to your commission. In the six months since the commission was established, this is one of the first times it has heard from the *victims* of RCMP Security Service harassment.

The Revolutionary Workers League believes that the Security Service is guilty of enormous crimes against democratic rights. Those crimes, we will show, result from the very nature of the task assigned the SS by the government—which is to curb and even suppress the activities of those who hold dissident political views.

We will cite some of the ways in which the RWL has been victimized by the "dirty-trick" squads of the Security Service.

We will demonstrate that SS harassment of organizations like the RWL has no justification in law, and is based on undemocratic political concepts.

We believe the Security Service should be disbanded, and that the police criminals must be brought to justice without delay. The

RCMP's secret files on millions of Canadians must be opened, and the dossiers turned over to the victims. The victims of political police "dirty tricks" must be compensated. These views are founded in part on our own experience. So it is important to explain briefly exactly what the Revolutionary Workers League is, and what we stand for.

The RWL: What it is, what it wants

The Revolutionary Workers League was founded in August 1977 through the fusion of three organizations — the Revolutionary Marxist Group, the League for Socialist Action/Ligue Socialiste Ouvriere, and the Groupe Marxiste Revolutionnaire. The RWL is the section in Canada of the Fourth International, the international party of socialist revolution founded under the leadership of Leon Trotsky in 1938. We trace our origins back to the early Communist Party, before its Stalinist degeneration in the late 1920s.

We hold that this society needs to be reorganized on the basis of production for human needs, not for private profit. We think that a socialist society, based on collective ownership of the productive apparatus, economic planning, and workers control, will be qualitatively more democratic than the capitalist "democracy" we know today. As our founding *Statement of Principles* declares: "Revolutionary Marxists actively defend all democratic rights of the masses, including freedom of movement, of assembly, of belief, of speech, and all trade-union rights. Moreover, they seek to qualitatively expand all these rights in a workers state by ending the economic and political limitations imposed on them by the capitalist order." (See Appendix, p. 81)

We think that such a society will be achieved only through the struggle of the working class and its allies, organized independently of the capitalists and their political parties. That is why we support every move by the working people in the direction of independent labor political action. In English Canada, we give critical support to candidates of the New Democratic Party against the candidates of the Liberal, Conservative, and Social Credit parties. In Quebec, our members are active in the movement to found a workers party based on the unions.

On many issues our views are shared by many, if not most, Canadians and Quebecois. These issues include the right of every worker to a job; the right of the Quebecois to self-determination and to enact whatever laws they wish in defense of their language, culture, and national rights; the right of women to equal pay, abortion, and childcare; opposition to racism and support of the aboriginal rights of the Native peoples; support of the rights of immigrants, especially against undemocratic legislation like the new Law C-24; and opposition to Canada's membership in imperialist military alliances and Ottawa's complicity in efforts to frustrate the liberation struggles of oppressed peoples in southern Africa, the Middle East, Latin America, and elsewhere.

On the question of establishing socialism, however, we are in a minority. We seek to win a majority to our point of view.

We engage in a wide range of activities to explain our ideas and win support for our program. We hold public meetings and distribute leaflets, books, and newspapers. Our members participate in organizing demonstrations, such as the large demonstrations that opposed the war in Vietnam or that supported Quebec's right to legislate protection of the French language. Many of our members are active in the labor movement, and the movement for women's liberation.

We run in elections; for example, the RWL fielded candidates recently for the mayoralty in Edmonton, and in the provincial election in Manitoba.

None of these activities is illegal or undemocratic.

The Revolutionary Workers League and its predecessor organizations have never engaged in terrorism in any form, and have circulated books and pamphlets to try to convince others that it is ineffective and counterproductive.

The RCMP has never produced any evidence to show that we advocate or engage in violent or illegal activity.

But despite that fact, our organization — in common with other political parties, Quebecois nationalists, trade unionists, farmers organizations, Native activists, and others—has been subjected to a long campaign of harassment, disruption, and intimidation by the RCMP and other police forces in English Canada and Quebec.

In recent years, on various occasions, members and supporters of the RWL and its predecessor organizations have been subjected to police raids; their homes have been searched, documents seized.

Some have been jailed arbitrarily without charge, as during the

War Measures crisis. Some have lost their jobs because the RCMP and other police provided information on their political affiliations to their employers.

Members have been visited by police and threatened in attempts to gain information or to turn them into informers. Their relatives have been visited and bullied by police.

In at least two instances, attempts to infiltrate police informers into our ranks were uncovered.

Police have written anonymous "poison-pen" letters and circulated them to our members in efforts to stir dissension in our ranks.

Our offices have been broken into, and political files and subscribers lists have been stolen; there is every reason to suspect police involvement or complicity. We will briefly describe some of these incidents later in this presentation.

We have been placed on secret government blacklists. An immigration department blacklist of this type has just recently come to light. (See page 67)

All of these police actions are designed to hinder and prevent our organization from functioning legally and normally. They are an assault not only on our democratic rights, but on the rights of all Canadians and Quebecois.

In this presentation, we intend to explain our view of why the RCMP and other police forces conduct such activities, why they should be opposed, and what should be done to put an end to them.

The McDonald Commission: Part of the cover-up

First, however, we want to make clear that in our view, the purpose of this commission is not to expose the secret, undemocratic activities of the RCMP Security Service. And it will in no way remedy such practices.

The commission was set up only after the Quebec government had established the Keable inquiry into illegal RCMP actions. Its aim is clearly to provide a federal counterweight to the Keable inquiry. In his repeated attempts to quash the proceedings of the Keable inquiry, Solicitor General Francis Fox has used the existence of this federal commission to buttress his absurd claim that Quebec has no right to investigate evidence of illegalities committed by Ottawa's police on Quebec territory.

But what is the McDonald commission? Prime Minister Trudeau, hardly a disinterested observer, has stated that the commission's task is to propose ways to legalize practices of the RCMP that may at present be illegal. In this respect, the commission would be following in the footsteps already traced by the 1960s Royal Commission on Security. That commission, it will be recalled, helped to prepare the way for the establishment of the now-infamous Security Planning and Analysis Group — since revealed to be responsible for compiling illegal blacklists of civil servants, trade unionists, and members of a wide range of organizations for use by the federal cabinet.

The McDonald commission, since its establishment more than half a year ago, has held few hearings, still fewer in public. It says it may take years to issue its report. Meanwhile, the Trudeau government refuses to take any action to stop illegal practices by its security police or to prosecute the offenders, instead referring the mounting disclosures of police illegalities to the commission. The McDonald commission is a federal government vehicle for controlling information on RCMP practices.

More than a month ago, the commission announced that it was investigating up to 100 incidents of possible wrongdoing by the RCMP, including break-ins, illegal wiretaps, and mail openings. Reports in the news media indicate that the commission has been given an RCMP internal report prepared in the summer of 1977 by Supt. J.A. Nowlan, dealing with illegal actions of the RCMP that are not being investigated by the Keable inquiry. It has been offered, and presumably has agreed to accept, the transcripts of the Keable inquiry's secret hearings.

If this commission is to have any credibility, it must inform the victims of these police attacks, so that they may take appropriate legal measures. The commission should also allow the alleged victims of RCMP illegalities to be present during any investigation by the commission of those allegations. The Revolutionary Workers League formulated these requests in a letter to the commission on December 21, 1977.

We have been informed by the commission secretary, however, that if the commission finds evidence of police illegalities, its only responsibility is to inform the federal cabinet — which may well have authorized the illegalities in the first place. Moreover, the commission has failed to answer our request to be represented by counsel in any investigation of incidents involving our organization. Yet lawyers for the RCMP, the Quebec Surete, and Solicitor General Fox and his two predecessors, Messrs. Allmand and Goyer, participate in the proceedings of the commission, with the right to cross-examine witnesses. The client of each of these lawyers has something to protect, if not hide.

This commission, hand-picked by Ottawa, represents no one and speaks for no one except the Trudeau government. Consider the close political and personal ties each of the commissioners has with that government. The chairman, Mr. Justice David McDonald, is a former president of the Alberta Liberal Party, and a personal associate of Trudeau. Donald Rickerd is a former business associate and friend of Francis Fox. And Guy Gilbert, a member of the Quebec Liberal Party, is known to have urged Fox to run for Parliament and to have personally contributed to his campaigns. Even the secretary of the commission, H.R. Johnson, is a former advisor to Prime Minister Trudeau, once employed by the Privy Council office. The commission has been aptly compared to an "old boys' network."

Will a commission like this be inclined to shed full light on the RCMP's activities, to release information that could seriously embarrass the government — in short, to reveal the truth about the secret, undemocratic activities of Canada's political police? To ask the question is to answer it.

The real task of the commission is to deflect, cover-up, and legitimatize secret police activity — just like its forerunner, the Royal Commission on Security.

The Revolutionary Workers League has no illusions in this commission's intentions or utility. Our presentation is designed only to use its public hearings as a forum, however limited, to expose the RCMP's attacks on democratic rights, especially those practices and policies of which we have been the direct victims.

'Security' spying: Terrorism is not the issue

The police actions whose disclosure forced the creation of this commission had nothing to do with countering illegal activities like espionage, terrorism, kidnapping, and the like.

This point is underscored by the ridiculous attempts of RCMP officials, in testimony before the Keable inquiry and this commission, to portray the targets of their dirty-tricks squads as being linked with terrorism or espionage.

The following four examples are the only "evidence" they have presented to prove their contentions. All four fall apart at the first contact with the facts.

1. The break-in at the Agence de Presse Libre du Quebec, police said, was designed to procure a letter that outlined plans for terrorist actions in Quebec to be carried out with possible Cuban government collaboration.

The actual letter, made public by the Keable inquiry, had a quite different content. The authors, Jacques and Louise Cosette-Trudel, who were implicated in the kidnapping of James Cross in October 1970, *renounced* terrorism, saying they were "overwhelmed" and "revolted" by their actions in the October Crisis, and had come to believe in "the necessity of putting a stop to armed agitation."

Once in possession of the letter, the RCMP tried to suppress it. An RCMP officer analyzing the letter in a report for his superiors wrote that it "could easily impress many people in this milieu."

As for the alleged Cuban connection, it was equally unfounded. The Cosette-Trudel letter spoke of Prensa Latina's desire to compile files on Canadian politicians — a simple task for the Cuban government press agency, since not only is there a Cuban embassy in Ottawa, but Prensa Latina itself had recently opened a bureau in Montreal!

2. Chief Supt. Donald Cobb, a participant in the APLQ break-in, told the McDonald commission about a "Parizeau spy ring," through which Parti Quebecois leader Jacques Parizeau attempted to gain information on government operations. The story would be laughable — what political party with the mass support of the PQ wouldn't have access to such information? — if it weren't for Cobb's absurd attempt to suggest that the PQ leaks such information . . . to France. Rather than demonstrating the dangers of French espionage in Canada, a common enough theme with some federal ministers, the incident simply shows the pathetic lengths to which the RCMP is prepared to go in its efforts to paint the PQ, and Quebec nationalism, as something "foreign" and "disloyal."

3. Then there is the famous barn the Mounties burned down, allegedly to block a meeting between the "FLQ" and the U.S. Black Panthers. Few newspapers have bothered to point out that the "barn" was in fact a rather well-known social and cultural

center for Quebec nationalists; for a period it even quartered a jazz ensemble, the Jazz Libre du Quebec—a sinister outfit indeed.

4. As for the Mounties' dark hints of an alleged aircraft hijacking plot they were worried about in 1972, it seems that now they'd rather not talk about it. Recent news reports indicate that three of the five "FLQ" members plotting the hijacking, including the one who initiated the proposal, were RCMP agents. In other words, the "hijack" plot may well have been a massive provocation designed to once again put Quebec under the War Measures — in the middle of a federal election campaign.

Far from confronting a wave of terrorism, it now turns out that during this period the RCMP was actually attempting to stimulate "FLQ" violence through such means as issuing a forged "FLQ" communique attacking Pierre Vallieres' renunciation of terrorism. This communique, replete with inflammatory appeals to "reach our goal with arms" and for "violent revolution to liberate us from capitalist tyrants," was written to counter the views of those trying to *stop* terrorism.

Most interesting, there is the information of Security Service agents themselves that of the three "FLQ" cells they claim existed in 1972, *all* had members who were police, and *the police may even have controlled these cells.* One is led to speculate on the personnel and the real intentions behind those who were said to be plotting an airplane hijacking during the 1972 federal election campaign—a plot that is even said to have included plans to kill someone.

The latest information, we suggest, when put together with various disclosures about the events of October 1970 since the October crisis, would indicate the need to *reopen the dossier on the War Measures crisis.* Were there police agents provocateurs in the groups that kidnapped James Cross and Pierre Laporte? How did Laporte die? Did Ottawa know the kidnappings were planned before they happened? If so, why did it not move to prevent them?

And behind all these unanswered questions, there is the big *political* question about the October crisis: Why was the War Measures Act invoked?

Was there really an "apprehended insurrection"? By whom?

We believe that a serious investigation that had access to all the relevant police and government files would find that the invocation of the War Measures Act was itself a provocation—not by terrorists, but by the Trudeau government, designed to intimidate the Quebecois with a massive display of federal force, to show them what would happen if they chose to exercise their right to self-determination. The kidnappings were simply a pretext.

The relevance of such an investigation is driven home by the prime minister's recent threat to once again wield the War Measures bludgeon.

The October crisis is invoked again and again by the federal government as justification of its campaign against so-called subversives. Yet Ottawa is plainly afraid—deadly afraid—of any independent inquiry into the circumstances surrounding that fateful chapter in the country's history. It is now before the Quebec courts for the fifth time in two months, seeking to frustrate the Keable inquiry's timid encroachments on this forbidden subject.

Yet the issue cannot be avoided: any investigation of the RCMP Security Services and police repression in recent years must confront the events of October 1970. The pattern of evidence raised by subsequent events—the break-in at the APLQ, the theft of Parti Quebecois membership lists, the spying on the public sector unions, and so on—leads back inexorably to those unanswered questions about the War Measures crisis.

As to the APLQ break-in whose disclosure set in motion the current revelations, there are some important questions concerning it that just beg for answers. One that has yet to be aired in any satisfactory way, we believe, has to do with the functions of Robert Samson, the RCMP officer who first broke the story. Samson, it will be recalled, was on trial in 1976 for bombing the home of an executive of a supermarket chain, during a strike by the company's employees. Why was an RCMP agent bombing the boss's house? Did he think the FLQ and the Black Panthers were about to hold a meeting there? *Or was the RCMP trying to frame the union for the bombing?*

No, it was not the struggle against "terrorism" that preoccupied the RCMP in these incidents, or in all the other questionable activities attributed to the Security Service. Their real concern was the radicalization of the *mass* organizations of the Quebec working class and the nationalist movement—especially the most militant leading wing of these movements—in this politically volatile part of the Canadian state. Likewise in English Canada—from surveillance of the New Democratic Party to compiling reports on trade-union activities; from spying on university students to using information from medical records to intimidate and blackmail radicals—the real aim of Canada's political police is to investigate, harass, and disrupt a wide range of organizations whose only "crime," in the eyes of the Trudeau government, is that they are capable of expressing opposition to the status quo.

'Subversion': an ideological crime

We maintain that the principal, overriding function of the 1,900-strong Security Service of the RCMP is to restrict the rights of free speech and freedom of association in this country, by curbing and even suppressing the activities of those who hold dissident political views.

The police activities cited earlier were carried out in the name of combatting "subversion." But what is "subversion"?

Democratic tradition, backed by an impressive body of jurisprudence, has long held that criminal liability attaches only to specific actions, not one's views. It is true that in every capitalist democracy this principle is often violated in practice, and in many countries in law as well.

But the people of Canada and Quebec have a long history of opposition to attempts to frame people on the basis of their political views. For example, there was the long struggle for repeal of Section 98 of the Criminal Code. Section 98, adopted after the Winnipeg General Strike, outlawed membership in any association said to advocate or defend the use of force to bring about governmental, industrial, or economic change. Anyone who attended meetings of such an association, distributed its literature, or spoke out in its support, was presumed to be a member. This law was used to frame up and jail labor militants, including leaders of the Communist Party. Mass pressure forced its repeal in 1936.

A more recent example of public opposition to thought-control legislation and trials is the public support manifested for the defendants in the Quebec "sedition" trials under the Public Order Act, 1970, which was modelled very closely on the old Section 98 of the Criminal Code.

But in recent years there has been a sustained effort by political authorities to enlarge the role of the RCMP in policing dissent, utilizing a sweeping definition of "subversion" so broad that it could encompass any organization or individual holding dissident opinions. A notable attempt in this direction was made by the forerunner of the McDonald commission, the Royal Commission on Security. In their report, published in censored form in 1969, the commissioners wrote:

"Subversive activities need not be instigated by foreign governments or ideological organizations; they need not necessarily be conspiratorial or violent; they are not always illegal." (page 2)

What is "subversion," then? The commissioners acknowledged they were unable to devise "any satisfactory simple definition," but attempted to come up with one anyway: ". . . subversive organizations or individuals usually constitute a threat to the fundamental nature of the state or the stability of society in its broadest sense, and make use of means which the majority would regard as undemocratic." (page 3)

Not illegal, not violent, not foreign-inspired, but "a threat . . . to the stability of society." That expresses rather precisely the police mentality that lurks behind every attempt to proscribe or otherwise restrict the expression of certain political opinions. And who is to determine what "the majority" regards as "undemocratic"? A government can claim that "the majority" regard a strike as "undemocratic." The commissioners deliberately avoided the normal expression "make use of illegal means," in order to substitute the whim of a government for the criteria of the law.

Under cover of this sweeping definition of "subversion," the commissioners described the "main security threats" to Canada as being posed by "international communism" and by "some elements of the Quebec separatist movement." (page 5)

The commissioners even tried to combine the two "threats," red-baiting the movement for Quebec independence.

". . . there is no doubt about communist and Trotskyist interest and involvement in the [separatist] movement," they wrote. "Both groups have established 'autonomous' Quebec organizations as somewhat transparent attempts to exploit separatist sentiment; members of both have achieved positions of influence in at least some of the separatist groups and agencies, helped by the often bitter factionalism within the movement itself. For these reasons alone it seems to us essential that the Canadian security authorities should pay close attention to the development of these particular elements of the separatist movement." (page 8)

The attempt to portray the Communist Party as a supporter of Quebec independence is rather forced. The CP has never supported the Quebec independence movement, but instead champions "Canadian unity."

As for the Ligue Socialiste Ouvriere (LSO), as the Trotskyist organization in Quebec was then called, it was indeed defending Quebec self-determination — not in a covert, conspiratorial manner, as the commission suggests, but openly, energetically, and enthusiastically.

At that time (1969), members of the LSO and the youth organization in sympathy with it, the Ligue des Jeunes Socialistes (LJS), were participating in the struggle in Saint-Leonard to establish a single, secular French-only school system, a struggle that is not yet won in Quebec. They were fighting attempts by the Union Nationale government to legislate increased protection for English, the language of privilege in Quebec. They were active in building the student movement: in 1968, they were leading participants in the massive upsurge of student revolt that shook the CEGEPs (junior colleges) throughout Quebec in support of free tuition and jobs.

None of this was illegal. Nor was it undemocratic. On the contrary, the struggles for students' rights and to defend French-language rights were attempts to deepen democratic rights.

Yet because of its support of these actions, the Ligue Socialiste Ouvriere did receive "close attention" from the police security forces, as recommended by the federal royal commission. In fact, just a year after the commission's report, federal authorities demonstrated their desire to defend democracy against threats from the LSO by jailing election officials of the LSO's candidate for the Montreal mayoralty. Arthur Young and Penny Simpson, respectively campaign manager and agent, were held for over a week during the War Measures crisis before being released without charge.

The "separatist movement" and the Ligue Socialiste Ouvriere were not the only "threats . . . to the stability of society" to be singled out by the royal commissioners. The commission also proposed more stringent measures against the employment of homosexuals in the public service, defended continued "security" surveillance of university campuses, and recommended rejection as immigrants of persons who (*inter alia*) might at some time in the previous ten years have been members of "subversive or revolutionary organizations." (page 51)

In the name of safeguarding Canada against "subversion" and "revolution," the commission was prepared to countenance a great deal in the way of secret police activity. It is widely forgotten today, for instance, that the commission *recommended* police surveillance of the mails "for activities dangerous to the security of the state" — a vague enough pretext. (page 103)

We emphasize: In order to arrive at a pretext for political police spying and disruptive operations, it was necessary for the royal commission to develop a concept of "subversive activities" that went beyond the commission of illegal acts—and that even excused illegalities by the state authorities.

The commission's definition of "subversion" was never given legislative sanction. But in succeeding years the government went very far in attempts to give it a cover of administrative authority.

The Security Service 'mandate': the goal is thought control

In a speech in Parliament on October 28, 1977, Solicitor General Francis Fox described the various legislative steps by which the RCMP Security Service developed its present apparatus and scope of operations.

The speech is remembered mainly because of Fox's disclosure, inserted almost imperceptibly into his text, of "the alleged offences committed in 1973 and involving property belonging to the Parti Quebecois"—that is, that the RCMP had broken into an office and stolen PQ membership lists and other documents.

But the speech merits attention for another reason: it remains to this day the most coherent attempt by the Trudeau government to explain its position that (to paraphrase Barry Goldwater) "illegality in defense of national security is no vice."

"One of the first steps in the formulation of new guidelines for the security service of the RCMP," said Fox, "has been the adoption by Parliament in 1974 of a new definition of the expression 'subversive activities' that is to be found today in the Protection of Privacy Act which amended certain aspects of the Official Secrets Act. It was then decided that this definition constituted a solid starting ground from which the role of a good security service could be defined more precisely."

The Protection of Privacy Act of 1974 (since it legalized wiretapping and similar practices it might more aptly be called the Invasion of Privacy Act) amended the Official Secrets Act to include the following definition of "subversive activity" (Section 16(3)):

"(a) espionage or sabotage;

"(b) foreign intelligence activities directed toward gathering intelligence information relating to Canada;

"(c) *activities directed toward accomplishing governmental change within Canada or elsewhere by force or violence or any criminal means*;

"(d) activities by a foreign power directed toward actual or potential attack or other hostile acts against Canada; or

"(e) activities of a foreign terrorist group directed toward the commission of terrorist acts in or against Canada." (emphasis added)

Section (c) in particular appears to be aimed at domestic dissent. The wording leaves considerable scope to judicial interpretation of such phrases as "activities directed toward" and "or elsewhere." That is, the legislation could be used to legally frame up individuals or organizations on the basis of intentions, not specific acts, or to prosecute opponents of dictatorial regimes elsewhere.

But in so far as the legislation in question refers only to explicitly "criminal" acts, it could hardly provide legal justification for surveillance of the Revolutionary Workers League, or of most other organizations that have been victims of the Security Service's domestic harassment and disruption tactics.

The RWL and its predecessor organizations, for example, have never been indicted or convicted for any violent or criminal activity. The RWL does not propose to accomplish its aims through illegality.

The government apparently felt the parliamentary mandate was insufficient. In a secret order-in-council on March 27, 1975—to the best of our knowledge not revealed publicly until Fox's speech in October 1977—the federal cabinet "defined the mandate of the security service," as Fox put it.

This "mandate" went considerably further than any legislation ever submitted to Parliament, let alone the people of Canada and Quebec as a whole. According to Fox, it authorized the RCMP "to discover, monitor, *discourage, prevent and thwart* the activities of certain individuals or certain groups in Canada and carry out investigations about them when there are reasonable or likely grounds to believe that they are carrying out or do intend to carry out. . . ." The solicitor general then paraphrased the definitions of "subversive activities" in the Official Secrets Act, with the following significant addition: "the use *and encouragement* of the use of force or violence or any other criminal means, the *provocation or the exploitation of civil disturbances* in order to take part in any of the above-mentioned activities." (emphasis added)

There are two things in particular to note about the cabinet's instructions to the Security Service.

One is the addition of the new clause, authorizing police operations against organizations and individuals who, in the police view, "encourage" the use of force, violence, etc., or that "provoke" or "exploit" civil "disturbances." These terms are so open-ended that they could apply to almost any conceivable form of political or social protest. If the cops smash a picket line, for example, can't the resulting "civil disturbance" be blamed on the union that erected the pickets? Couldn't it be argued that in setting up a picket line the union members "encouraged" or "provoked" the resulting disorder? Police thinking of that nature is not unknown, as many union members can testify.

Also to be noted in the cabinet's instructions is the phrase "discourage, prevent and thwart." Is this the Trudeau government's explicit endorsation of "disruption tactics," which of course were in use long before adoption of the cabinet directives? The cops who carried away all the files of the APLQ and the Quebec Political Prisoners Defense Movement were, after all, simply "preventing and thwarting" these organizations from functioning. We will return to this point later.

The cabinet directive of March 27, 1975 goes to the heart of the present operations of the RCMP Security Service—and for that matter, other forces that collaborate with the RCMP in their "antisubversive" witch-hunts. It gives police virtually *carte blanche* to carry out their "dirty tricks." Yet, let it be emphasized, this cabinet directive, which goes considerably further than any parliamentary act in encouraging such activity, was adopted behind the backs of the Canadian people.

Since its adoption, the cabinet's definition of the SS "mandate" has croppped up in other places. For example, *Socialist Voice*, the English-language biweekly that reflects the views of the Revolutionary Workers League, recently obtained a copy of a secret

Immigration Department "manual" designed for departmental internal use. The manual added the new definitions of "subversion" in May 1975 to its "criteria for refusal of immigrants and non-immigrants on security grounds."

We have gone to some lengths to describe the thinking of the federal government and its agencies on this question, since it is clear that these concepts of "subversion" have been developed precisely to give some cover of "legitimacy" to police action against the Revolutionary Workers League and its predecessor organizations.

Both Prime Minister Trudeau and Solicitor General Fox have on several occasions in recent months singled out "Trotskyists" as worthy subjects for police surveillance. Ontario Attorney General Roy McMurtry told the provincial legislature in December that the RCMP explicitly described the League for Socialist Action as "subversive" in discussions with his deputy attorney general.

We have been accused, tried, and convicted by the government—not for any criminal actions, but solely on account of our political opinions, such as our support for Quebec independence.

By labeling us "subversive," the government and its police agents try to present our members and supporters as opponents of democracy, and advocates of violence and terrorism.

But the government and their police forces know very well that the Revolutionary Workers League is a legal political organization.

We do not advocate terrorism. In fact, we have had occasion—for example, at the time of the October 1970 kidnappings and in the 1972 Munich events—to polemicize strongly against such tactics in the newspapers that reflect our views. The position of our world organization, the Fourth International, on this question is well-established. Advocacy of terrorism is incompatible with membership in the Revolutionary Workers League.

As for the suggestion that we oppose democratic rights, nothing could be further from the truth.

Revolutionary socialists are not only defenders of those democratic rights that already exist. We favor their extension and qualitative enlargement.

The workers state and constitution we advocate will recognize the unrestricted rights of free speech; freedom of movement, assembly, and religion; and a multiparty system and free elections.

The workers government that we are fighting to establish will support complete legal status for *all* political organizations and parties, including those that oppose socialism and the constitution of the new state, so long as they do not take violent *action* against the democratically-established laws. In our view, dissolving the capitalist police forces and replacing them with a popular militia under democratic control—a traditional goal of socialism—will safeguard the gains of the socialist revolution far better than "dirty trick" squads can ever protect capitalism.

A more complete exposition of our views on this question can be found in a public statement entitled *Socialist Democracy and the Dictatorship of the Proletariat*, adopted in May 1977 by the United Secretariat of the Fourth International.

What the government is doing with its concept of "subversion" is to attempt to fashion a new category of crimes, crimes of thought and ideas. In this way it empowers its "security" police to define in effect which thoughts are acceptable, and which aren't.

This attempt must be rejected by all supporters of democratic rights.

Legal or illegal: the case of the disappearing distinction

Much stress has been placed by some critics on whether SS operations of the kind recently exposed were legal or illegal. This commission itself has emphasized that its concern lies mainly with the prevalence of "illegal" actions by the SS.

We contend that by the very nature of political policing, the distinction between "legal" and illegal actions tends to disappear.

As we have seen, the Security Service's crimes against free speech have no justification in law. Their formal "authority" rests largely on cabinet ukase; it has in the main never been submitted to Parliament, let alone to a democratic consultation of the Canadian people.

Many aspects of SS operations, moreover, remain a closed book. Even the parliamentary committee charged with overseeing the RCMP is denied information on the SS budget.

What about the specific *actions* of the Security Service? Is it possible to establish a limited authority for the SS that somehow does not infringe on democratic rights?

First, let us note that those responsible for formulating and defending the SS policy show no such insistence that the RCMP remain within the limits of legality. In urging that the Security Service be beefed up, the 1969 royal commission stated: "A security service will *inevitably* be involved in actions that may contravene the spirit if not the letter of the law, and with clandestine and other activities which may sometimes seem to infringe on individuals' rights. . . ." (page 21, emphasis added)

In his statement last October announcing the RCMP theft of Parti Quebecois property, Solicitor General Fox cited these remarks, and stressed that (as he put it) "the royal commission did not say that a security service must never be involved in any actions 'that may contravene the spirit if not the letter of the law.' "

Fox described a "dilemma" rooted in the very nature of political police activity. "At precisely what point," he asked Parliament, "should a security service refrain from taking action that it thinks important to meet its responsibility for national security in order to avoid any possibility of contravention of even the letter of the law?"

The solicitor general even suggested that this "dilemma" should give the public cause to sympathize with the SS's action in breaking into the PQ files. It was done, you see, in the interests of "national security."

Thus, in the opinion of the minister directly responsible for the RCMP, *raison d'etat* — "national security" — could justify the commission of patently illegal actions by the police sworn to uphold this country's laws. To this day, Fox refuses to admit that the PQ break-in was necessarily "illegal."

Prime Minister Trudeau has, if anything, gone further. At a news conference last October 28 the prime minister carried the doctrine of *raison d'etat* to its logical limits. If the police have to break the law in pursuing those whom they consider subversives, the prime minister said, "There is a very simple thing to do. It is to make such types of surveillance permissible by the RCMP or by whatever security agency you have and this is what we have asked of the McDonald Commission . . . to advise the Government on. . . ."

These gentlemen at least have the merit of frankness. We ask only one thing: that if they are to defend lawbreaking by the police, and to urge the legalization of what is presently illegal, they should have the elementary decency to stop posing as defenders of democracy and "law and order" and stop slandering their victims as advocates of force and violence.

Let us be clear: in our view, the RCMP Security Service is guilty of crimes, enormous crimes against Canadian laws and the democratic rights of Canadians and Quebecois. Those responsible for these crimes should be brought to justice, and punished with the full rigor of the law.

But a deeper issue is at stake. We agree with the prime minister and the solicitor general: by its very nature police surveillance of political dissent or potential dissent, and attempts to "discourage, prevent and thwart" the expression of dissent, will inevitably involve law-breaking by the police—at least, in any capitalist democracy that still claims adherence to the "rule of law." The difference is that we oppose such surveillance and disruption of free speech, while the government supports and encourages it.

Forged communiques, break-ins, mail openings, theft, blackmail—that is what the prime minister is asking this commission to ratify.

Dissent and subversion: how real is the difference?

Some critics of RCMP practices have tried to steer a "middle course," urging that a distinction be drawn between dissent and subversion. Worried that police practices increasingly infringe on the right of dissent, they argue for a narrower definition of "subversion," and seek official support for broadening the bounds of "legitimate" dissent—presumably dissent that does not somehow threaten the "foundations of the state" or the "stability of society," to use the words of the 1969 royal commission (abridged) report.

The New Democratic Party leadership in particular has leaned heavily on that kind of argumentation. This is not a new argument with the NDP. It need only be recalled that one of the three members of the Royal Commission on Security was M.J. Coldwell, a former CCF-NDP leader. Coldwell apparently subscribed entirely to the reactionary thought-control concepts of the commission's report, if he wasn't himself their direct author. The government naturally attached considerable value to his support.

In reality, it is not possible to make a meaningful distinction between dissent and subversion.

It is clear from the government's definition that "subversion" implies outlawing the expression of some forms of dissent. To attempt to distinguish subversion and dissent is to accept the criminalization of some dissent.

Once the legitimacy of thought control activity has been adopted and ratified, the logic of *raison d'etat*—the "interests of national security," as it is often called in Canada—takes over. Police actions otherwise condemned as illegal can become "legal," at least in the minds of their perpetrators. (It is no accident that the cops involved in the APLQ break-in, testifying before the Keable inquiry, were unclear about the legality of their actions. The one thing they all agreed on was that they were acting in the interests of "national security." That, for them, was sufficient.)

Trudeau, one of the more conscious representatives of his social class, knows this very well. Hence his oft-stated doctrine of "ministerial ignorance." He knows that police political spying inevitably involves lawbreaking. His position that he does not want to know the details of such activities might more aptly be termed a doctrine of ministerial *complicity*. Those who formulate the policy are responsible for the results.

The police use their "antisubversive" mandate to intervene in all areas of actual or potential opposition to government policies. A case in point is the RCMP's attempts to justify its "surveillance" of the Parti Quebecois and the New Democratic Party.

In a typical statement, Solicitor General Fox told Parliament October 31, 1977: ". . . if by any chance there are people in the Parti Quebecois or any other political party with Maoist, Trotskyist or other political tendencies, it would obviously be advisable for the security services to keep an eye on such groups to serve the best interests of both the Canadian and Quebec governments."

Fox's allusion to "Trotskyists" in the PQ is absurd, of course. While we support Quebec's independence, we are opponents of the PQ, as anyone acquainted with our views knows. We don't join the PQ, and we urge the formation of a workers party based on the unions in order to fight this capitalist party.

Fox's shabby pretext that the PQ must be spied on because of the existence of Trotskyists is no more convincing than the 1969 royal commission's suggestion that the LSO had to be investigated because it supported Quebec separatism.

Likewise with respect to the New Democratic Party. The RCMP initially attempted to excuse its alleged three-year investigation of the NDP with the claim that it was only investigating the left-wing "Waffle" caucus. Since that sounded unconvincing to many, it then argued that it was investigating the Waffle caucus because of the presence in it of Trotskyists. The truth is, the RCMP was investigating *the NDP*, and in doing so it violated the democratic rights of members of the NDP. The state has no business intervening in the internal affairs of the NDP or of any political grouping. We are appalled that NDP leaders have failed to see this point and to protest the RCMP's intervention in the strongest possible terms.

These police methods recall the salami tactic: cutting off the opposition slice by slice. In Quebec it began as surveillance of the "FLQ"; but the disruptive tactics soon were directed against the whole spectrum of the nationalist movement. The War Measures Act was invoked, we were told, to stop "an apprehended insurrection." By the "FLQ"? Within days a Liberal cabinet minister Jean Marchand was denouncing the trade union-sponsored Front d'Action Politique, the main opposition to Mayor Drapeau's party in the Montreal elections, as "a front for the FLQ."

An attack on one quickly becomes an attack on all. That is why, very early in the history of the radical movement, the principle was established that whatever their political views, all victims of police repression must be defended.

Who is to draw the line? Who is to determine what is a "legitimate" target for police spying, and what is not? How radical must you be before you are "subversive"?

RCMP the real subversives

The police code-word for political spying is "surveillance"—as if it were confined to information-gathering. Trudeau has encouraged this misconception with his frequent statements to the effect that there is nothing wrong with the police keeping files on the views and activities of millions of Canadians.

But files are compiled to be used—as they were under the War Measures in October 1970, when hundreds of innocent persons were arrested and held for days or weeks, and thousands of homes were raided. In the end, there were few indictments; only a handful of persons were convicted of anything. Yet thousands suffered: their reputations were harmed, many lost their jobs—all because the police had files on them as persons to be watched because of their views or associations.

Will we see a repetition of this experience — or something worse? Only two weeks ago Trudeau threatened to again invoke the War Measures Act. Isn't it *his government* that is actually

threatening the use of force, against the people of Quebec?
When the federal cabinet authorized the RCMP to "discourage,
prevent and thwart" the activities of individuals and
organizations, it not only gave the green light to much more than
"information gathering," it made clear that police disruptive tactics enjoy the support of the highest levels of government. What
those tactics can involve was indicated by the APLQ break-in.
Despite the cops' initial claims that they were trying to foil
terrorist actions, the real purpose of the operation was to smash
the news agency and the political prisoners' defense committee
that shared the building with the APLQ. As Capt. Roger Cormier
of the Montreal police described it, in testimony before the
Keable commission: "We wanted to prevent them from functioning. . . . It was in our interest to destroy the two movements."
That's why documents taken in the break-in were not returned
but were later destroyed, police say. The material included all the
organizations' files, contact lists, subscribers lists, and addresses.
The Revolutionary Workers League and its predecessor
organizations have also been the target of police "disruption tactics." The following small sample of incidents involving our members provides further evidence of the kinds of methods employed
systematically by the police against an organization like
ours—which, we repeat, has never been indicted or convicted for
criminal activity.
1. Katie Curtin is a graduate student in Montreal and author of
the book *Women in China.* Curtin was fired from a job at the 1976
Olympics; her employer said security officials had called her a
"risk to national security."
Curtin took her case to the Commission des Droits de la Personne, seeking damages for loss of her summer earnings. In
testimony before the commisssion RCMP officers confirmed she
had been fired on the basis of RCMP files. But when the commission requested the files, Solicitor General Fox intervened with
an affidavit under Section 41(2) of the Federal Court Act,
claiming absolute immunity from disclosure on grounds of
"national security."
Thus the RCMP, acting as judge, jury, and executioner, have
convicted Katie Curtin as a "risk to national security," deprived
her of her job, and then denied her any means of seeing the
evidence or defending herself — on the grounds of "national
security." Catch 22.

Curtin is not alone in her dilemma. Other members of the Revolutionary Workers League, including members of the former
Groupe Marxiste Revolutionnaire, similarly lost their Olympics
jobs on the basis of police political files; police admit that at least
20 and perhaps as many as 150 persons suffered a similar fate.

2. Will Offley, a member of the RWL in Vancouver, came to
Canada in the late 1960s from the United States. A draft evader,
he renounced his U.S. citizenship in order to demonstrate his opposition to the war in Vietnam. Offley, who later joined the
League for Socialist Action, applied for Canadian citizenship and
was turned down without explanation.

In 1975 John Rodriguez, MP, asked the government on behalf
of Offley: "As of March 1973, was the League for Socialist Action
designated as a subversive organization?"

The Hon. Mitchell Sharp, president of the privy council, issued
a written reply, published in *Hansard* November 5, 1975, at page
8883. Sharp said that "no minister, agency, or level of government
declares organizations subversive." The minister misled the
House.

Immigration department internal guidelines recently brought to
light show that at the time Sharp spoke, the LSA was indeed listed
as a "communist controlled organization," and thus "subversive"
according to the government's criteria.

As in the case of Katie Curtin, the blacklist, presumably drawn
up by the RCMP, is secret; neither the LSA nor Offley (who could
reasonably presume that his membership in the LSA was the cause
of his refusal of citizenship) had any means of confronting their
accusers and answering the charge.

Offley has since obtained his citizenship, but only by dint of a
long, difficult campaign.

3. In April 1974 three trade-union activists were fired at Flyer
Industries, a Manitoba government-owned corporation. Two of
the three persons fired were active socialists; one was a member of
the Revolutionary Marxist Group, a predecessor of the RWL. On
November 3, 1977 Siegfried Maurmann, a former president of
Flyer Industries, admitted to the press that the RCMP had been
called into the plant offices to check a list of company employees
for suspected "subversives." Maurmann said that two of the three
men fired "had earlier been named by the RCMP as having
Marxist persuasions." Howard Pawley, a former attorney general
of the province, has confirmed to the press that the RCMP was in-

volved in the firing of these militants.

As a petition signed by leaders of the labor movement and the NDP in Manitoba states: "The nature of the RCMP-Flyer management collaboration in 1974 suggests a systematic and widespread surveillance by the security branch [of the RCMP] against politically dissident groups and individuals in the unions and on the left. It also suggests that the RCMP has acted in the service of corporate management to deprive workers of their jobs and of their democratic rights."

Before unions became widespread, employers circulated blacklists among themselves in order to weed out militant workers from their factories. By informing bosses of their employees' political affiliations, isn't the RCMP reviving these infamous tactics?

4. Brenda Dineen, LSA candidate for mayor of Winnipeg in 1974, ran second, receiving more than 6,000 votes. Shortly after the election a member of the Winnipeg Police Department began undercover surveillance of the LSA. Christie Brian Rush, alias "Chris Mathieson," expressed interest in joining the LSA. He attended its public activities and at one point was observed copying down names from the organization's mailing list. It was later discovered that he was a member of the police department.

Confronted by this evidence, Deputy Mayor Bernard Wolfe defended police infiltration tactics. "This type of activity," he told the press, "can determine what goes on that is to the disadvantage of the established governments."

It is not known if the RCMP was involved in this action by the Winnipeg police: but there is no reason to think they would have opposed it. It is well known that the SS works in close collaboration with local police "red squads," often assigning "tactical operations" to them.

5. In April 1971, a few months after the War Measures crisis, Montreal police called John Lejderman, a laboratory technician and member of the LSO and the Ligue des Jeunes Socialistes, into the office of the company where he worked and accused him in front of his boss of being a member of the FLQ, then an illegal organization. No charges were laid. When Lejderman protested this smear attack, he was assured by both the Montreal police department and the Quebec Justice ministry that there was nothing irregular in such police conduct.

A few days after his protest to Quebec Justice Minister Jerome

Choquette, police raided Lejderman's home with a search warrant alleging possession of "writings, pamphlets, books, etc., which advocate rebellion against the government of Canada relative to Section 60 of the Criminal Code." They carried away personal property, including a passport and similar seditious documents, and refused to allow any of the property to be listed by Lejderman or his companion. When Lejderman protested these procedures, he was assaulted by a detective, taken to a police station, and detained in a cell for two hours. Again, no charges were laid.

When police returned Lejderman's belongings in July 1971, they inadvertently included the results of their search. A list of more than 60 names culled from Lejderman's papers and letters was accompanied with notes like: "Sheet with names and telephones to be checked with Bell Tel.," and "Sheet for information on the Jeunes Socialistes." (Rapport general de la police de Montreal no. 906-138, May 7, 1971)

During this period, which followed the emergency measures enacted in October 1970, other members of the LSO and LJS were arrested on various occasions and held by police for up to 12 hours without charge. They were illegally interrogated and photographed. While holding Therese Faubert in custody, police took her keys, entered her apartment, and removed several items including minutes of LJS membership meetings.

6. In 1972-73, political differences in the League for Socialist Action/Ligue Socialiste Ouvriere gave rise to the formation of several organized tendency formations, or caucuses. While the internal political debate was proceeding, many members in branches in Vancouver, Edmonton, Winnipeg, Toronto, Ottawa, and Montreal received anonymous letters through the mails purporting to be sent from members of one or another minority tendency, and attacking various leaders of the LSA/LSO.

The league's executive secretary, John Riddell, was the target of an extensive campaign of letters containing various attempts to discredit him. For example, in a letter found on delegates' chairs at the Young Socialists' convention in December 1972, reference was made to the fact that Riddell had "sought psychiatric aid."

Other letters, postmarked in Toronto, accused leaders of the LSA of insufficiently opposing the views of one tendency in the Fourth International, which at that time was also going through an intense political debate.

Still other letters, in French, attempted to stir up animosity between English and French speaking members in Montreal. When one such letter, postmarked in Montreal in August 1972, failed to get any response, it was followed by another in late September 1972 that attempted a more subtle line of attack using the same theme.

Members took it for granted that the police were involved. This suspicion has now been virtually confirmed by recent disclosures of RCMP attempts during this same period to provoke dissension in Quebec nationalist circles through circulation of forged "FLQ" communiques. In announcing the latter, has the federal solicitor general really "cleared the slate" of RCMP illegalities, as he alleges?

7. Between August 20 and August 25, 1971, while the LSA/LSO and Young Socialists were holding a widely publicized socialist activists' conference at the University of Waterloo, the headquarters of the LSA in Toronto was broken into; membership lists and political files were stolen. Money was left untouched. The operation had all the earmarks of a police operation.

That is only a small sampling of the kind of harassment members of our organization have been subjected to by the RCMP and related security forces. There are literally dozens of similar incidents we could cite, covering just the last ten years.

In no case have our members been convicted of any criminal offense associated with these incidents. The police aim has clearly been to intimidate members and disrupt the functioning of the organization. Many members have been damaged materially and intimidated as a result of this harassment.

These police activities continue to this day. Since the founding convention of the Revolutionary Workers League in August 1977, members of our organization in several cities have been approached by the RCMP and asked to inform on the RWL.

Persons acquainted with our organization who are not members have told us that when they applied for citizenship, for example, they were extensively questioned by the RCMP about the RWL or its predecessor organizations.

Such police tactics, to say the least, are not calculated to help us win new members and supporters.

That is why we say it is not us but the RCMP—and its "political masters" in the government—who are the real subversives in this country. They are subverting our democratic rights, and the rights of the Canadian and Quebecois people.

Is the RCMP 'out of control'?

Although they may often violate "the spirit if not the letter of
the law," these current police practices are sanctioned at the
highest levels of government. Moreover, they are based on a long
tradition of police activity in this country. Above all, they are
rooted in the historical development of Canadian capitalism, and
in the evolution of the Canadian state into a modern imperialist
power.

The Royal North West Mounted Police, the RCMP's forerunner, was established originally in order to suppress the Native and
Metis peoples in Western Canada — to make the West white and
English-speaking. Its early recruits won their spurs by breaking
strikes among the superexploited workers, many of them Chinese
immigrants, building the Canadian Pacific Railway. Later, the
force was used to round up opponents of Canada's involvement in
imperialist wars — the Boer war, and the first and second World
Wars — especially in Quebec.

The RCMP played an important role in suppressing the Winnipeg General Strike and in organizing the anti-sedition witch-
hunts that followed that strike and the post-World War I labor upsurge. Becoming the main political police force after the First
World War, the RCMP made a vocation of harassing members of
the Communist Party, other radicals in the labor movement, immigrants, and Native people.

In recent years it has placed increased emphasis on combatting
the nationalist movement in Quebec. It is under the aegis of Ottawa's "antiseparatist" campaign that the RCMP has grown to the
dimensions we know today. And with it have grown the secret
operations of the Security Service, with its reported staff of 1,900
officers.

There is nothing qualitatively new about the recent actions of
the Security Service. They are not aberrations. The RCMP is not
"out of control" of the government. SS activities flow from the
very nature and function of the RCMP as a repressive force.

What is new, however, is the political context of the current
revelations.

Over the years, Canada's rulers have gone to great pains to
cultivate a favorable public image of "the Mounties." For labor
militants, Native peoples, and socialists, the contrast between the
myth and reality was always too great to be credible. But critics of

the RCMP usually found it difficult to get a hearing, especially in the extended period of capitalist expansion and Cold War that followed World War II.

What touched off the current rush of revelations and criticism concerning the RCMP was, above all else, the Parti Quebecois election victory, the enormous impetus it has given to the independentist movement in Quebec, and the resulting rise in tensions within the Canadian state apparatus as a whole.

The crisis of "national unity" necessarily entailed a crisis for the police agency that enforced that "unity"—especially since official propaganda has long portrayed the Mountie on his horse as a symbol of Canada itself! Today, hundreds of thousands of "Canadians" want to leave Canada and have their own country, Quebec; millions more seriously question the existing constitutional arrangements. They are no longer prepared to tolerate the undemocratic agencies and practices that stand in the way of their national self-determination. Moreover, in both Quebec and English Canada, more people than ever before question that the capitalist system is capable of solving the pressing social problems confronting them. They no longer accept the rationale for political police spying.

The crisis of the RCMP is essentially a *political* crisis, bound up with the institutional crisis wracking the entire Canadian state. And it is another demonstration of the increasing incompatibility between democratic rights and the needs of monopoly capitalism.

The ruling class faces a major problem: just when they most need to beef up their secret police and other specialized agencies of repression, there is more and more *political* opposition to such measures.

This commission has been given the task of justifying a still wider political role for the police. We will not speculate on its probable success.

But one thing is clear: efforts by the government to justify police "dirty tricks" and repression against the left by invoking a "terrorist" threat simply will not wash.

It may have worked in 1970; Ottawa was able to take advantage of the confusion caused by a couple of kidnappings. But subsequent events—such as the "sedition" trial of labor leader Michel Chartrand—demonstrated that the real purpose of the mass arrests and troop movements had little to do with catching the kidnappers. And there are still a great many unanswered questions about the government's role in the October crisis.

As indicated by his New Year's threat to use the War Measures, Trudeau hopes to play this card again. In the last analysis, he hasn't much choice: as long as he is committed to upholding Canadian "unity" he cannot renounce the use of force. But the public excuses for repression of this kind are wearing thin.

An example is the explanation proferred in defense of the Parti Quebecois break-in. Trudeau told a news conference that "you have to put yourself in the context of the times," and cited the need to "track down the kidnappers and assassins. . . ." Fox elaborated in his report to Parliament: "It was authorized and carried out in the absolute conviction that its sole object was to promote the security of Canada given the political and social climate prevailing in 1973."

But what was the "political and social climate" at the time of the October 1972 APLQ break-in and the January 1973 PQ break-in? During the previous year former "FLQ" leaders like Pierre Vallieres (and, as we noted, Jacques Cosette-Trudel) had renounced terrorism publicly. Actions attributed to the "FLQ" were at an all-time low. No one was doing any kidnapping, unless it was the police who sequestered radicals in motels, roughing them up to induce them to become informers. "FLQ" communiques were being written by the RCMP.

Meanwhile, bitter labor struggles like the *La Presse* strike had aroused support for radical union manifestos; and in the spring of 1972 Quebec had experienced a massive upsurge of the labor movement in protest against the jailing of the leaders of the three main union federations. The mass movement had recovered from the shock and disorientation produced by the War Measures; *and it was precisely this revival of mass action that spelled an end to isolated terrorist actions.*

The RCMP knows very well that it is this kind of mass movement that poses the real threat to the established order, and not the isolated actions of small terrorist-oriented groupings.

How can democratic rights be defended?

Democratic rights are not threatened by small terrorist groupings, whether they call themselves the "FLQ" or whatever. Nor are democratic rights threatened by the mass organizations the working people have forged in defense of their economic and political interests.

But the democratic rights of the people of English Canada and Quebec *are* threatened, and are being undermined, by the political police of the RCMP Security Service. And behind the SS stands the political authority of the Trudeau government, which committed the biggest act of political terrorism in the history of Canada when it invoked the War Measures Act in 1970.

That is why we say:

The Security Service should be abolished.

Its files should be opened and the dossiers turned over to the victims, their rightful owners.

Victims of "dirty tricks" squads should be compensated for the damages they have suffered.

All police surveillance, harassment, and disruption of the labor movement, the Quebec nationalist movement, Native peoples, and political parties should be ended. Stop the policing of political dissent!

The Revolutionary Workers League believes that police political spying will not end until capitalist rule itself is ended. The capitalists have too much to hide, too much to fear, to dispense with this vital tool of their system.

Not only do capitalist governments constantly whittle away at democratic rights—but, as the War Measures showed, they are quite prepared to sweep those rights aside with the stroke of a ministerial pen.

Working people cannot rely on the government, its courts, and its laws to defend their rights. The only guarantee of those rights is their collective strength and vigilance, and readiness to fight in their own defense.

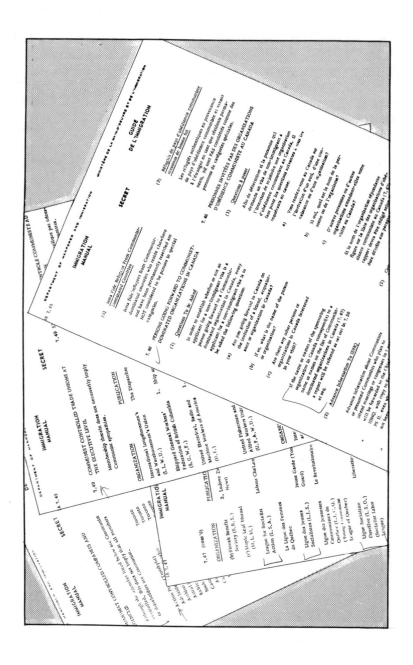

SECRET

IMMIGRATION MANUAL

GUIDE DE L'IMMIGRATION

DEPARTMENT OF MANPOWER AND IMMIGRATION
MINISTÈRE DE LA MAIN-D'ŒUVRE ET DE L'IMMIGRATION

7.49 COMMUNIST CONTROLLED TRADE UNIONS AT THE EXECUTIVE LEVEL

Membership therein does not necessarily imply Communist sympathies.

PUBLICATION — The Dispatcher

ORGANIZATION
International Longshoremen's and Warehousemen's Union (I.L.W.U.)
Shipyard General Workers' Federation of British Columbia (S.G.W.F.)
United Electrical, Radio and Machine Workers of America (U.E.)
United Fishermen and Allied Workers Union (U.F.A.W.U.)

7.47 (cont'd)
ORGANIZATION
(b) Slovak Benefit Society (S.B.S.)
(c) Maple Leaf Mutual (M.L.M.)
League for Socialist Action (L.S.A.)
La Ligue des Femmes du Québec
Ligue des Jeunes Socialistes (L.J.S.)
Ligue des Jeunesses Communistes du Québec (L.J.C.Q.) (Young Communist League of Québec)
Ligue Socialiste Ouvrière (L.S.O.) (Socialist Labor League)

PUBLICATION
Labour Challenge
Jeune Garde (Youth Guard)
Le Révolutionaire
Liberation

(5) Bona Fide Refugees from Communist-Dominated Countries

Bona fide refugees from Communist-dominated countries who have been permanently resettled are NOT considered to be persons in special categories.

7.46 PERSONS GOING FORWARD TO COMMUNIST-DOMINATED ORGANIZATIONS IN CANADA

(1) Questions To Be Asked

In order to establish whether or not an applicant for a non-immigrant visa is a person going forward to a Communist-dominated organization in Canada, the applicant for a non-immigrant visa is to be asked the following questions:

(a) Are you going forward to Canada on the initiation of a friend, acquaintance or organization in Canada?

(b) If so, what is the name of the person or organization?

(c) Are there any other persons or organizations in Canada interested in your visit?

If the name or names of persons or organization in Canada correspond to a name on the list of Communist-dominated organizations in Canada (7.47 et seq.), a report will be referred as set out in 7.48.

(2) Advance Information to IHHQ

Advance information about Communist or presumed Communists who plan to attend meetings or organizations will be forwarded to IHHQ. IHHQ, with copy to the Chief of the R.C.M.P. D., even when such persons are not being sponsored.

(3) Réfugiés de pays d'obédience communiste reconnus de bonne foi

Les réfugiés authentiques en provenance de pays d'obédience communiste et à l'étranger de relations ne résidents permanents, NE sont PAS considérés comme des personnes de catégories spéciales.

7.46 PERSONNES INVITÉES PAR DES ORGANISATIONS D'OBÉDIENCE COMMUNISTE AU CANADA

(1) Questions à poser

Afin de déterminer si la personne qui demande un visa de non-immigrant a l'intention de visiter une organisation d'obédience communiste au Canada, il faut poser les questions suivantes à tout requérant en cause:

a) Vous rendez-vous au Canada sur l'invitation d'un ami, d'une connaissance ou d'une organisation?

b) Si oui, quel est le nom de la personne ou de l'organisation?

c) D'autres personnes ou d'autres organisations s'intéressent-elles votre visite au Canada?

Si le nom de l'organisation répondante figure sur la liste des organisations d'obédience communiste au Canada, un rapport devra être rédigé selon le paragraphe décrite aux paragraphes...

(2) ...

4. Ottawa's Secret War on Democratic Rights

The following articles describe some of the methods used by Canada's political police in their attempts to harass political opponents of the government and otherwise curtail democratic rights.

These articles first appeared in Socialist Voice, *a biweekly newspaper that reflects the views of the Revolutionary Workers League. Subscriptions may be obtained by writing to* Socialist Voice, *25 Bulwer Street, Toronto M5T 1A1. One year (24 issues) $5.50*

a. Immigration blacklist

After the 1973 military coup that toppled Chile's Popular Unity government, thousands of Chileans fleeing rightist repression sought refuge in Canada. Many were turned down by Ottawa.

Civil liberties groups, churches, and trade unions appealed to the Trudeau government to open Canada's doors to the Latin Americans.

They were met by a wall of official silence.

Why have so few victims of right-wing military dictatorships been allowed into Canada?

And why did Ottawa refuse to allow a noted left-wing academic personality like Andre Gunder Frank to visit this country in 1977 for a university seminar?

Answers to these questions may lie in secret immigration de-

Opposite page: Sample pages from secret immigration department manual

partment documents recently leaked to *Socialist Voice* and civil-liberties lawyers in the Toronto area.

The documents show that behind the backs of the Canadian people, the federal government has conspired to block the entry of persons to Canada on the sole basis of their political views. And it has compiled secret blacklists of "communist controlled" organizations, unions, and businesses in Canada to screen visitors invited by those groups.

Section 7.16 of the secret *Immigration Manual*, issued to visa officers and immigration agents at all entry points into Canada, lists "Criteria for Refusal of Immigrants and Non-Immigrants on Security Grounds."

The section, dated May 1975, instructs department officers to refuse entry to "persons who, there are reasonable grounds to believe, would be likely, if admitted to Canada, to engage in . . . the use or the encouragement of the use of force, violence or any criminal means, or the creation or exploitation of civil disorder. . . ."

The wording is virtually identical to a cabinet order-in-council that has been used in recent years to authorize RCMP harassment in Canada of radical political groups, unions, Native organizations, and Quebec nationalists.

The cabinet order, made public last October by Solicitor-General Francis Fox, was adopted March 27, 1975, barely one month before the immigration manual's section 7.16, "criteria," was issued.

It has never been given parliamentary sanction. Fox revealed its existence when he told Parliament about the RCMP's 1973 theft of Parti Quebecois files.

The secret immigration regulations apply similar criteria to persons trying to enter Canada.

How does the department decree that a would-be visitor or immigrant is likely to create or exploit "civil disorder" in Canada? Is it, as seems likely, on the basis of secret police files in his or her country of origin, made available through the collaboration of the RCMP?

In addition, a list in the manual that appears to have been compiled in 1972-73 cites more than 60 organizations and publications as "communist controlled." Among them are the League for Socialist Action/Ligue Socialiste Ouvriere and the Young

Socialists/Ligue des Jeunes Socialistes. The LSA/LSO was a predecessor of the Revolutionary Workers League.

Others on the blacklist include the Communist Party, the Canadian Party of Labor, the now-dissolved Fair Play for Cuba Committee, various Maoist organizations, and many ethnic organizations.

Also listed are the names of publications and businesses thought to be linked to these groupings, including "Vanguard Bookstore, Toronto," associated with the LSA/LSO.

Yet another section lists four "communist controlled trade unions at the executive level."

The manual makes clear that any persons wishing to enter Canada, whether as visitors or immigrants, who are sponsored by or associated with any of the organizations or businesses cited on this secret blacklist, will be closely screened and possibly turned down.

These organizations have never been informed of the existence of the immigration department political restrictions and blacklists, still less given any chance to defend themselves against the implied label "subversive."

The immigration department blacklists are not likely the only ones. How many other departments of the federal government have similar lists?

The immigration blacklist is further proof that RCMP political "surveillance" involves much more than information-gathering. The secret files compiled by Canada's political police are being used to bar political dissidents, and dissident viewpoints, from Canada.

It is not only refugees from right-wing dictatorships who suffer from such practices. The Canadian people, deprived of acquaintance with these people and from hearing their views, are also among the victims.

January 23, 1978

b. 'Don't get caught'

On the CBC television program "The Fifth Estate" September 20, 1977 members of the RCMP were quoted as saying that illegal wiretaps and break-ins are "common practice." They described their participation in such activities. Locksmiths listed on the cops' payroll as "informers" described how they often assist RCMP agents on some of the more complex assignments.

One of the officers interviewed by "The Fifth Estate" recounted how he and another cop once were listening to the radio while sitting in on a wiretapped conversation when they heard then RCMP Commissioner Maurice Nadon on the radio denying such practices existed. "There we were, sitting there with all the equipment in front of us. . . ."

The two officers who agreed to be interviewed (their actual words were read on the program by professional actors, to maintain their anonymity) indicated that they had decided to speak out because they feared the RCMP brass would disown them if their activities were revealed, thereby leaving them alone to face the rap. They cited recent statements by retired RCMP Deputy Commissioner William Kelly, an unofficial spokesman of the force, that illegal activities were the work of "overzealous" junior officers.

According to senior CBC producer Ron Haggart, "this type of surreptitious entry is widely used in all types of investigations."

The following are excerpts from a Socialist Voice *transcript of the "Fifth Estate" program. Questions and comments are by CBC reporter Eric Malling.*

CBC: How many of these break and enters would you have made in a year?

RCMP officer: Well, it's hard to say what an average is. Sometimes I guess we've done three a week and another time two or three months would go by and we wouldn't do any. . . .

CBC: ...Did you have any authorization to be in there at the time?

RCMP officer: Ah, who can authorize a break-in? A break-in is a break-in, I suppose. At the time I didn't feel it was morally wrong, it was an investigative method that was necessary. And break-ins are common practice. And you know they're sort of standard fare, you know, an accepted way of investigating any type of crime. . . .

CBC: What's actually in the manual? What does it say about breaking and entering?

RCMP officer: Well, the operations manual doesn't set it out in terms of breaking and entering, it's in terms of major and minor installations. But it just goes without saying you can't install a bug without going in. . . .

CBC: When a major installation is taking place, how do you organize it? How do you lay the whole thing out?

RCMP officer: It's a big investigational step and it's thoroughly discussed by the brass and there's a lot of preparatory work. You've got to go down and break into the building several times as a preliminary step, and there's great pains taken in setting it up. I've been in several major installations and I'd say there have been anywhere from 20 to 50 men involved in one way or another.

CBC: The Mounties are probably the only lock-pickers who have to fill out a form and get permission before breaking into a place. This is it. It's called the preliminary technical survey. It must be completed and approved by a senior officer before a bug is placed in somebody's home or office. The form requires detailed descriptions about a place, descriptions available only to someone who's been inside.

Here are some of the questions they have to answer. How is it decorated? What's the furniture like? How is the wiring laid out? Will the city police cooperate if the Mounties get caught?

The snoopers are supposed to get paint samples so they can patch and conceal the hole where a bug has been put into the wall. They even study the habits of the occupants and the neighbors, even following the children on the street. So when the bug is being planted, a team of up to 40 Mounties can follow and if necessary stop anyone who might come in.

All of this must be done illegally before even an authorized listening device is placed. The Mounties might go in up to six times just to get the information to fill out this form. This is not the work of a few zealots. The permission comes from the top. It is the top officers in Ottawa who have set out this formal procedure for the men in the field. . . .

Former Deputy RCMP Commisioner William Kelly: I would say that if there is authority to bug then I think there must go along with that the authority to enter the premises one is going to bug.

CBC: But it's not really specified in the law.

Kelly: It is not specifically specified in the law. That is right.

CBC: You stood before one of the graduating classes of that entry and wire tap school on a Friday afternoon and gave them their final address and written behind you in huge letters on the blackboard were the words, Don't get caught.

Kelly: That is true. The idea is not to get caught. The point is, to get caught is to make the operation ineffective. . . .

CBC: Dr. Ross McGuinness is a general practitioner in the small farming town of Shubenacadie, Nova Scotia. He signed a committal order against a Mountie almost 20 years ago and since then he's been plagued by investigations and charges, including one of performing an illegal abortion. He's been acquitted on all of them. McGuinness has also had a number of break-ins. Once he returned to his clinic late at night to find the lights on, evidence of a break-in, and an RCMP car pulling away. The photostat machine was still warm. The detachment in Truro dismissed his complaint. But the Inspector there made a curious blunder.

McGuinness: Basically he accused me of trying to put false charges or false statements against the RCMP. Because he said at that hour, there was no squad car anywheres near my area. The odd part about it was that I'd mentioned neither to he nor to the constable at what hour the thing had taken place.

CBC: McGuinness also found a bug in his office through which police could share his patients' most intimate problems.

McGuinness: It was just up here under the ceiling—above my desk. Now the, it was just a microphone there. Now in there, in here, in the washroom next door to my office, up under here . . . was a transmitter . . . from which a wire led to the bug and another little thing went up sort of like an aerial affair. So apparently this thing would transmit outside the building. . . .

CBC: We went through a city in this country with an RCMP wiretap man who told us about the bugs in hotel rooms, in offices, jail cells, even the rooms in police stations where lawyers interview their clients. He knew exactly where they were because he'd put them there and in most cases he'd entered surreptitiously to do so. . . .

RCMP officer: It isn't a little hanky-panky thing we do at the constable level. It's an established format that we've been trained to do and for senior officers to turn around and say they know nothing about it is—I'm very anxious to see them take the stand and explain that away to me. . . .

CBC: It's not hard to imagine . . . the consequences of planting that bug in a doctor's office in a small village in Nova Scotia. The tales of family disputes, the confessions of fears, anxieties, and inadequacies, the rumors and gossip about other people, all of this was shared not only with the GP but also with someone else's tape recorder. The Mounties deny that they did it, but they are after all the only police force in that part of Nova Scotia, and it was a sophisticated installation of high technology. . . .

We talked to many Mounties and former Mounties in the preparation of this program. You heard the actual troubled words of two of them. And if those two are typical, then there have been thousands of surreptitious entries by stealth into properties we consider our own. It's a regular routine method of investigation, accompanied by all the usual bureaucratic trappings of form filling and prior approvals from on high. All these surreptitious entries into homes to look around, into offices to rifle through files, cannot possibly be the spontaneous enthusiasm of a few zealots in the field. The zealots, we're afraid, live elsewhere.

October 24, 1977

c. Warren Hart:
RCMP-FBI double agent

Blacks, Native people, and immigrants fighting government repression in Canada in the early 1970s faced an additional, unknown obstacle—a secret agent of the RCMP and FBI in their own ranks.

Warren Hart, a Black currently working for U.S. Navy intelligence near Washington, has told Tory MP Elmer MacKay and the *Toronto Sun* that between 1971 and 1975 he worked as a paid informer for the RCMP Security Service. The Mounties paid him $900 a month and expenses.

A former FBI agent in the Black Panthers, Hart says that during his four and a half years in Canada:

● He became personal bodyguard and confidant of Rosie Douglas, a Black militant from Dominica then fighting Ottawa's attempts to deport him from Canada. Using bugged apartments, body microphones, illegal mail openings, and even fancy cars equipped with mikes and tape recorders, Hart says his assignment was "to report on any and every one attending any of the meetings or contributing money" to Douglas's legal defense. Douglas was finally deported in 1976.

● Benefiting from his association with Douglas, Hart travelled across Canada several times reporting to the RCMP on labor groups in Montreal, Blacks in Nova Scotia, Native militants, and student and Haitian immigrant groups.

● Hart accompanied Douglas on at least two tours of the Caribbean, at RCMP expense. On returning, he says, "I was debriefed by the CIA." His reports on Black activists in the West Indies were also passed on to British Intelligence.

● Hart was present—and secretly taped the proceedings—during meetings Douglas had with the B.C. NDP legislative caucus, with NDP MP John Rodriguez—and even with then Solicitor General Warren Allmand, who was in charge of the RCMP. With respect to the latter incident, Hart indicates the political police mentality: "I was told to tape the conversation. . . . Most of the RCMP was under the impression Mr. Alman (sic) is a Communist."

Hart says he later told Allmand he had taped him, but Allmand didn't seem surprised. Why should he? Surely the solicitor general was aware of the RCMP agent in Douglas's entourage.

Hart was more than an "informant" for the RCMP, as MacKay and the big-business press imply. He was a provocateur. As Gary Cristall reports below, Hart attempted to get Native militants to commit illegal or violent actions.

Cristall's testimony is confirmed by Toronto activists in the Rosie Douglas defense effort. They told *Socialist Voice* that Hart, as Douglas's "bodyguard" often argued—unsuccessfully—that marshals at Douglas's public meetings should be armed illegally with guns.

"We simply pointed out that that would give the cops a pretext to raid the meetings and arrest participants—including many non-citizens," said Liz Barkley, an executive member of the St. David's NDP riding association.

"Rosie always agreed with us, and that settled the matter," she added.

Hart's testimony provides a revealing insight into the nature of RCMP collaboration with the FBI, the CIA, and the British secret service.

And it leaves some unanswered questions.

● According to the *Toronto Sun* Hart, while working for the FBI, sent Black Panther members to Montreal "to work with the FLQ." The Mounties say they burned down a barn to prevent an FLQ-Black Panther meeting. Were they also setting up meetings between the two groups? And why—in order to frame both of them?

● Rodriguez, the New Democratic MP, says he was probably bugged by Hart at a meeting he attended in Toronto in 1975 to discuss defense of Blacks and immigrants against physical attacks by the ultraright Western Guard. A trial of Western Guard leaders in Toronto that just concluded heard testimony that an RCMP agent in the Guard participated in, and sometimes initiated these attacks.

● Above all, the evidence that the RCMP was obstructing and undermining Rosie Douglas's fight against deportation points to the need to reopen the Douglas case. Douglas should be allowed to return to Canada.

And the RCMP files should be opened—to reveal all the secret activities of Warren Hart, and of all the agents like him.

March 6, 1978

d. Portrait of a provocateur

VANCOUVER—"I was an eyewitness to attempts by Warren Hart, confessed RCMP spy, to get British Columbia Natives to use violent tactics," Revolutionary Workers League member Gary Cristall told the press here February 27.

"It was a classic case of an agent provocateur—a police spy attempting to direct the struggle of oppressed militants in a violent direction. Hart's aim was to provoke actions that the police could easily suppress, arresting or killing radical leaders and discrediting the movement."

Cristall is a former member of the Revolutionary Marxist Group (RMG), which was active with the League for Socialist Action (LSA) in the campaign to defend Rosie Douglas from deportation. (The RMG and LSA were among the organizations that fused last summer to form the RWL.)

Cristall said he had worked with Hart on several occasions. "Hart was known to us as Clay Heart, nicknamed 'The General.'

"I remember Douglas and Hart made a cross-country tour of Canada in the summer of 1975. Douglas wanted to meet Native militants. He hoped to promote an alliance between Natives and immigrants to fight racism and political repression.

"I helped Douglas set up some meetings when they were in Vancouver in August 1975.

"Hart drove a late-model Lincoln Continental, with licence plates from an eastern U.S. state. He tried to give me and others the impression the car was stolen. He said he had picked it up for several hundred dollars and could get anyone a similar deal. He hinted he had links with a Black Panther 'auto theft ring' and said even the car registration would check out as valid.

"Now we know why. The car was probably RCMP or FBI issue, or at least protected."

Cristall described a trip he took with Douglas and Hart and two Native militants to the Mt. Currie reservation about 160 kilometres north of Vancouver.

"Mt. Currie was the site of a prolonged confrontation between Natives and the B.C. government in 1975 over the issues of fishing and hunting rights. A logging road had been cut through the reservation without Native permission. The Natives set up a series of roadblocks until the RCMP busted them on July 18, arresting dozens.

"Many of the Natives were frustrated and there were intense discussions on which direction to take the struggle. I attended meetings that included Douglas, several American Indian Movement (AIM) members, and Hart.

"I remember Hart claiming in these meetings that he had a lot of military training, and that he had done security work for the Black Panthers. He spent a lot of time talking to Native militants about military tactics, specifically dynamiting bridges. He said he had access to dynamite, and also to AK-47 rifles that he said Black veterans had brought back from Vietnam."

In no case did the Native militants fall for these provocations, Cristall said.

Similar incitements to violence by this RCMP agent probably occurred many times on this 1975 tour, Cristall pointed out.

"That was a time of growing rebellion by the Native peoples. In 1974 Anicinabe Park in Kenora was occupied; and there were the Cache Creek events in B.C. In 1975 there was the Mt. Currie blockade, the Batoche conference of Metis and Natives in Saskatchewan, and the Grassy Narrows conference.

"An RCMP report issued in July 1975—in the midst of Hart's cross-country tour—called the Native liberation movement 'the number one threat' to 'national security.' "

But it was RCMP provocateurs like Hart who posed the real threat to the security of Native people, Cristall said. And to the security of Blacks and immigrants, he added.

"While Hart the RCMP agent was personal bodyguard to Rosie Douglas, Douglas was in the middle of the Black immigrant community's efforts to fight the government's racist Green Paper on immigration."

"It is outrageous," said Cristall, "that Douglas was railroaded out of the country on the basis of RCMP reports that he was a 'threat to national security' while an RCMP agent, infiltrating Douglas's defense campaign, was fomenting violence behind his back."

March 6, 1978

e. RCMP collaboration with racists

TORONTO—Leaders of the Western Guard group here have been convicted on charges arising out of window-smashing and swastika-painting attacks on Jews, Blacks, and radical organizations. But a major offender, the RCMP, has so far gone scot free.

On February 1, after a three-month trial, a jury found Donald Andrews and Dawyd Zarytshansky guilty of conspiracy to commit arson, possession of explosives, and conspiracy to commit mischief.

The prosecution's star witness was Robert Toope, a paid RCMP agent.

Toope testified that he became a member of the Western Guard in early 1975, under the direct supervision of the RCMP. On their instructions, he initiated or participated in more than 100 illegal actions by the extreme right-wing group in which homes, stores, synagogues, churches, and other buildings were damaged.

Among the targets were the Vanguard Bookstore (now the Louis Riel Bookstore) and the offices of Pathfinder Press, distributors of revolutionary socialist books, pamphlets, and newspapers.

Despite the presence of an RCMP agent in the Western Guard, the police always denied they knew who was responsible for these attacks.

"I knew I was breaking the law on every incident," Toope told the County Court jury.

Corp. George Duggan of the RCMP's security service told the court the RCMP would have paid Toope's legal costs and any fine if he had been caught.

Duggan admitted not only that the RCMP knew of the racist and anticommunist attacks (often in advance), but that it encouraged Toope to carry through with them.

The RCMP paid Toope between 300 and 500 dollars a month for 14 months, and financed all his expenses, including the cost of gas while he drove the car on these reactionary escapades.

In an obvious attempt to deflect criticism from Jewish organizations, the RCMP emphasized that the Western Guard members were charged with conspiracy to disrupt a soccer match involving an Israeli team during the 1976 Olympic Games. Toope's activities, police said, helped thwart these plans.

But the judge instructed the jury to acquit the defendants on that charge, saying there was not enough evidence to convict.

In fact, the RCMP's collaboration in trashing expeditions by this racist outfit has no justification.

The evidence of RCMP complicity in Western Guard violence and racism is a new element in the current disclosures of illegal activity by the RCMP security service.

Toope testified he made daily reports to Corp. Duggan. He rose within the Guard to the rank of "group leader," he said. During a three-month period he was effectively in charge of the Guard in Andrews' absence. This indicates that for a time *the RCMP was actually leading the Western Guard.*

Burning barns, setting bombs, stealing dynamite, writing "FLQ" communiques. Now, organizing window-smashing and swastika-painting. And the full story is only beginning to unfold.

February 20, 1978

RCMP agent Robert Toope participated in painting these racist slogans on Louis Riel Bookstore (then Vanguard Books) in Toronto.

Appendix

Statement of Principles
of the Revolutionary
Workers League

INTRODUCTION

On August 8, 1977, in Montreal, three revolutionary organizations—the Revolutionary Marxist Group, the League for Socialist Action/Ligue Socialiste Ouvriere, and the Groupe Marxiste Revolutionnaire—voted to unite their forces to build a single revolutionary organization. Its name is the Revolutionary Workers League/Ligue Ouvriere Revolutionnaire, the section of the Fourth International in the Canadian state.

The fusion convention was the culmination of an intense process of common work and political discussions between the members of the three organizations. All members had an opportunity to present their points of view, both in writing, in a joint discussion bulletin, and orally during meetings of the membership held in 10 cities in English Canada and Quebec. In the course of this democratic discussion, many questions that have divided the three organizations were clarified and a solid political basis was established for the new organization.

The following document, cited in the RWL brief to the McDonald commission, constitutes the principled political basis of the new organization. It does not pretend to be an exhaustive programmatic text. Its aim is to define the borders that separate revolutionary Marxists from the class enemy and its lieutenants in the workers movement. Within that framework, disagreements and debates are both legitimate and inevitable.

1

For more than a century the domination of the capitalist mode of production has posed before humanity the alternatives: Socialism or Barbarism.

Decaying capitalism has long been the central obstacle to social progress. Imperialism in its death agony can promise the world's peoples only further economic crises, famine, war, national and sexual oppression, and the erosion of democratic rights.

Since 1945 the threat of nuclear holocaust has put in question the continued existence of humanity itself. The uncontrolled disruption of the environment by anarchic capitalism poses a similar threat.

The only definitive solution to these problems is the elimination of capitalism and its institutions, and the establishment of collective social ownership of the means of production, rational economic and social planning, and the abolition of all forms of national, racial, and sexual oppression and privileges.

Thus, the fundamental task of revolutionary Marxists is to build a revolutionary party capable of leading the workers and their allies toward the overthrow of capitalism and the establishment of socialism.

2

"All talk to the effect that historical conditions have not yet 'ripened' for socialism is the product of ignorance or conscious deception. The objective prerequisites for the proletarian revolution have not only 'ripened'; they have begun to get somewhat rotten." — *The Transitional Program of the Fourth International*

Since World War I, this statement has been verified time and again. The world revolutionary process has experienced periods of rise and decline; its tempo has been uneven. But it has never ceased to be the central political fact of the epoch that opened with the Russian Revolution of 1917. The workers and poor peasants have repeatedly shaken the very foundations of the capitalist order.

The majority of these struggles have ended in setbacks and even in defeats. However, the responsibility for these setbacks lies not with the masses, whose revolutionary capacity remains intact, but rather with the treacherous policies of the old leaderships of the masses: the Stalinist and Social Democratic parties, and, in the oppressed nations, the petty-bourgeois nationalist parties. The hold that these bureaucratic leaderships exercise today over the masses constitutes the central political obstacle to the victory of the world revolution.

The necessity of building revolutionary Marxist parties and a revolutionary Marxist International flows from both aspects of this reality: on the one hand, the actuality of the revolution; on the other, the necessity for a revolutionary leadership that is able to win the overwhelming majority of the workers, poor peasants, and other exploited social layers to the revolutionary program, and thereby to assure the victory of the socialist revolution.

3

Capitalism has developed as a *world* economic system. It is illusory to believe that the much higher development of the productive forces that socialism entails can be achieved within the framework of a single country.

The division of the world into different states imposes a definite form on the revolutionary process. The proletariat must and can take power and *begin* to build socialism in the territories defined by different existing states. But the construction of socialism can be completed only on a world scale.

Proletarian internationalism is the political and theoretical reflection of this reality. Far from expressing a sentimental or moral outlook, proletarian internationalism is based on the objective unity of interests of the world proletariat and on the *strategic interdependence* of its struggles in the various countries and regions. Such internationalism becomes concrete and receives its highest expression in the international revolutionary party, the Fourth International.

4

The uneven development of world capitalism and the world revolution determines the different components of the struggle for world socialism.

In the *advanced capitalist countries* the immediate task of the proletarian revolution is to expropriate and disarm the imperialist bourgeoisie and place full power in the hands of the working class, the majority of the population in these countries. In the *colonial and semicolonial countries* capitalism is unable to accomplish even tasks that the bourgeoisie long ago achieved in the advanced capitalist countries. The elimination of famine and illiteracy, the achievement of national independence and unification: all are pressing tasks of the colonial revolution.

But these national and democratic tasks cannot be fulfilled if the revolution is contained within a bourgeois framework. Only the growing over of the revolution into a socialist revolution—with the destruction of capitalist as well as precapitalist social relations, and the tearing of the national economy out of the world capitalist market—can ensure the definitive solution of the national and democratic tasks.

This combination of democratic and socialist tasks determines the need for the colonial proletariat to take power in its own name while establishing under its leadership a close alliance between the workers and the urban and rural petty-bourgeoisie (who constitute the majority of the populations in many of these countries).

The logic of this outlook, which revolutionary Marxists call the theory of permanent revolution, has been confirmed many times since the victory of the Russian Revolution (positively in China and Cuba, for example, and negatively in Algeria, Indonesia, and elsewhere).

In the *bureaucratized workers states* (including the Soviet Union, the East European countries, and China) the bourgeoisie has already been overthrown and capitalist relations of production have been replaced by nationalized, planned economies. But political power has been usurped by a privileged bureaucracy, which uses its monopoly over political and economic decision-making to protect and reinforce its material privileges. Only the victory of the antibureaucratic political revolution can permit the full development of socialist democracy.

While ceaselessly struggling for the overthrow of the ruling bureaucratic castes in these countries, revolutionary Marxists unconditionally defend these states against all imperialist attacks and against any attempt to re-establish capitalism.

5

The international labor movement has long been divided be-

RWL Statement of Principles

tween reformists—who claim that the proletariat's aims can be realized through the institutional framework of the bourgeois-democratic state—and proponents of the revolutionary road to socialism.

The bourgeoisie has demonstrated time and again that if its system is fundamentally challenged, it will defy any hostile parliamentary majority to defend its class interests. Its principal means of defense is its state apparatus: the courts, jails, police, army, and administrative bureaucracy. This apparatus must be demolished by the working class and its allies and replaced by a state based on democratically-elected councils of representatives of the working class and its allies.

These councils will be democratically linked together at the national and, ultimately, international levels. They will function according to the principles of workers democracy, derived from the experience of the world proletariat since the Paris Commune of 1871.

6

The victory of the revolution can occur only through the active participation of the overwhelming majority of the population. Thus revolutionary Marxists reject all militarist, putschist, and terrorist illusions. The actions of a small revolutionary minority cannot substitute for the revolutionary mass action of the proletariat and its allies.

7

The entire experience of the international proletariat for 150 years demonstrates conclusively that while the "spontaneous" action of the masses is an element of prime importance in the struggle for power, it is not sufficient to ensure the victory of this struggle.

The program of the socialist revolution, which includes the theoretical principles of Marxism and the strategic heritage of several generations of class struggle, will not arise spontaneously from the masses.

Only conscious and permanent organization of the proponents of this program can assure its survival and elaboration. Only the organization of the proletarian vanguard in a Leninist revolutionary party, equipped with the revolutionary program and rooted in the masses, can prepare the masses for the seizure of power in the Canadian state.

The Leninist party brings together all the forces within the working class and the oppressed layers who struggle for the socialist revolution. Its basis of unity is active agreement with the program of revolutionary Marxism.

It is not monolithic because the very diversity of the class struggle produces a diversity of opinion within the vanguard itself. Its positions are adopted by majority vote after a full, democratic debate in which all its members participate.

But it must be a party of combat, unified in action. So the positions adopted by the majority are applied by all its members until collective practical experience confirms or invalidates these positions. This method of functioning, demanding the greatest democracy in the elaboration of the line and the greatest discipline in action, is historically known as democratic centralism.

8

"The Communists . . . have no interests separate and apart from those of the proletariat as a whole. . . . They always and everywhere represent the interests of the movement as a whole." — *The Communist Manifesto*

Every defeat of the working class, no matter what the issue, is a blow to the socialist revolution. The proletariat prepares itself for the revolution through a variety of struggles around partial and intermediate goals. Revolutionary Marxists support and participate in all struggles against exploitation and oppression and seek to contribute to their victory.

However, the intervention and the program of revolutionary Marxists are in no way limited to participation in these partial struggles. The old Social Democratic division of the program into a maximum program (the revolution, mentioned only on Sunday) and a minimum program (small reforms within the framework of the system) must be completely rejected.

But at present the majority of the proletariat does not understand the necessity of socialist revolution. And it will not be convinced by ritual and abstract calls to revolution. To bridge the gap between the masses' present level of consciousness and struggle and the revolutionary consciousness necessary for the socialist revolution, a *transitional program* must be put forward.

For revolutionary Marxists this means a program of demands that are rooted in the objective needs of the masses and their present level of consciousness but which, in the course of struggle for their realization, lead the masses to understand the necessity to destroy the bourgeois state.

Revolutionary Marxists are consistent fighters for the unity of the working class. They support and build trade unions and fight for the unions to incorporate and take up the demands of all workers, regardless of sex, race, national origin, or political belief. They advocate the workers united front against the bourgeoisie.

United actions with the reformist workers organizations can be especially important in ensuring the victory of specific struggles, facilitating the development of proletarian class consciousness, and building the workers' confidence in their own revolutionary capacity.

9

The Stalinist, Social Democratic, and trade-union bureaucracies seek to deflect the thrust of the class struggle toward various types of collaboration with the bourgeoisie and its institutions.

Just as they are consistent fighters for the unity of the working class, revolutionary Marxists struggle at all times for the complete political independence of the proletariat and its allies from all sections of the bourgeoisie. They systematically oppose all forms of class collaboration: "integration" of the trade unions into the administration of the capitalist economy or individual enterprises; political support to bourgeois parties or governments; alliances between workers parties and bourgeois parties with the objective of forming governments.

10

Revolutionary Marxists actively defend all democratic rights of the masses, including freedom of movement, of assembly, of belief, of speech, and all trade-union rights. Moreover, they seek to qualitatively expand all these rights in a workers state by end-

ing the economic and political limitations imposed on them by
the capitalist "order." They endeavor to demonstrate to the masses
that socialist democracy is qualitatively more democratic than
bourgeois "democracy."

11

The struggle to liberate women from the bondage in which class
society has placed them is a struggle to free human relationships
from the shackles of economic compulsion and to propel
humanity along the road to a higher social order.

The oppression of one half of humanity—the oppression of
women—is a central strategic concern for revolutionary Marxists.
The oppression of women in general and the institution of the
nuclear family in particular are integral to the capitalist system.

Women's oppression is a mainstay of capitalist economic
stability, both through the superexploitation of women workers
and through the role of women's domestic labor in maintaining
the labor force. Ideologically, capitalism is bolstered by the
reproduction of capitalist social relations within the family.

Thus, one of the first tasks of a victorious socialist revolution
will be to initiate the socialization of domestic labor as a means
toward abolishing the sexual division of labor.

While understanding that only the overthrow of the capitalist
system itself will create the material conditions for the full
equality of women, revolutionary Marxists support all struggles
against the oppression of women and participate in building the
independent women's movement.

The liberation of women is a fundamental task both leading up
to and after the socialist revolution. This must be fully recognized
by the proletariat and its vanguard in order to realize the complete unity of the male and female sections of the proletariat and
to maximize the revolutionary potential of the independent
women's movements that have developed on a mass scale in many
countries.

Together with heterosexual women, male and female
homosexuals—who constitute at least 10 percent of the adult
population of the advanced capitalist countries—are oppressed by
the institutions and sexist ideology of capitalist society. Revolutionary Marxists denounce and combat all forms of legal
and ideological discrimination against homosexuals.

12

By virtue of its economic, social, and political characteristics and of its place within the world capitalist system, Canadian capitalism is defined by revolutionary Marxists as imperialist. Thus, they unconditionally reject all forms of Canadian nationalism as reactionary. The task of the proletariat in Canada is not to struggle for "independence" from U.S. imperialism. It is first and foremost to struggle for the overthrow of the Canadian bourgeoisie. A central aspect of revolutionary strategy is the struggle against the oppression of Quebec.

The Canadian state is a prison house of peoples. An unremitting struggle must be waged in defense of the rights of francophones in provinces outside Quebec and against the brutal oppression of the Native peoples. The working class must defend the rights of immigrants and ethnic minorities in Canada.

Active solidarity with the foreign victims of Canadian imperialism—in the first place, the oppressed masses of Africa, the Caribbean, and Latin America, is likewise a priority of revolutionary Marxists.

13

Quebec is an oppressed nation within the Canadian Confederation. Although its economy is highly industrialized, unlike classic colonies, its development has been deformed by Canadian and American imperialist domination. The Canadian state denies Quebec the right to self-determination—its right to its own state. The Quebecois suffer severe economic, social, cultural, and linguistic oppression.

The struggle of the working class and of the Quebecois masses for national liberation has profound revolutionary implications for the entire North American continent. It creates structural instability in the Canadian state, threatening the very survival of this state as a separate imperialist power. The example of this struggle can reverberate even in the United States, especially among the oppressed nationalities that are an important component of that country's working class.

Revolutionary Marxists defend unconditionally the right of

Quebec to self-determination and the concrete expression of that right, the struggle for political independence. But they also emphasize that without the complete elimination of imperialist domination, national oppression cannot be eliminated.

Only the proletarian revolution can lay the basis for national liberation by accomplishing simultaneously the national tasks and the expropriation of capital. The working class is the only class that can lead this struggle for national liberation and for socialism to victory.

The Parti Quebecois is a bourgeois nationalist party which, at present, enjoys the massive support of Quebecois workers. Revolutionary Marxists struggle for the Quebecois workers to break politically with this party and with all bourgeois parties and to form their own political party, which would fight for a workers government.

14

In English Canada there is only one mass party that is based on the organized labor movement, the New Democratic Party. Revolutionary Marxists describe this party as a reformist workers party of the Social Democratic type. This distinguishes it from the Liberal, Conservative, and Social Credit parties, which are parties controlled directly by the capitalist class and which function as its principal political instruments. This definition likewise distinguishes the NDP from the bourgeois nationalist Parti Quebecois.

But the NDP is in no sense a workers party from the standpoint of its program. It is completely committed to the preservation of the private property system and the bourgeois state. Its fundamental role is to represent the particular interests of the conservative trade-union bureaucracy.

The NDP can never be transformed into a vehicle of struggle for socialism. It is the principal obstacle to the socialist revolution within the organized workers movement in English Canada.

However, the hundreds of thousands of workers who currently follow the leadership of the NDP should not be identified with this rotten leadership. This leadership must be politically defeated through the building of a mass revolutionary workers party that will win the allegiance of the majority of the proletariat, including those who follow the NDP. The building of the revolutionary workers party in English Canada therefore requires flexible application of the united front tactic towards the NDP.

15

The victory of the socialist revolution requires an international program, an international strategy, and thus an international organization of the proletarian vanguard. These have always been the goals of all those who considered themselves revolutionary Marxists, including Marx, Engels, Lenin, Luxemburg, and Trotsky. These goals were inscribed in the program of the Communist International.

Today, alone among the various tendencies that claim the Marxist and Leninist heritage, the Fourth International functions as a worldwide organization. The struggle to build the Fourth International as a mass international revolutionary party is inseparable from the building of mass revolutionary parties in every country.

—Adopted August 8, 1977

'The enemy's on the look-out for your secrets,' says a poster now being sold in Quebec. It is modelled on familiar wartime posters.

Further Reading

Un Dossier Noir sur la Police Politique, published by the Ligue des Droits de l'Homme, 3836 rue Saint-Hubert, Montreal. 1978. 16 pages. no price listed.

An Unauthorized History of the RCMP, by Caroline Brown and Lorne Brown. James Lorimer & Company, 1978. 193 pages. $2.25.

The Assassination of Pierre Laporte: Behind the October '70 Scenario, by Pierre Vallieres. James Lorimer & Company, 1977. 192 pages. $6.95.

Against Individual Terrorism, by Leon Trotsky. Pathfinder Press, 1974. 23 pages. $.50.

Socialist Democracy and the Dictatorship of the Proletariat (resolution of the Fourth International). Vanguard Publications, 1978. 31 pages. $.75

Democracy and Revolution, by George Novack. Pathfinder Press, 1971. 286 pages. $5.45.

Prospects for a Socialist Canada, edited by John Riddell and Art Young. Vanguard Publications, 1977. 128 pages. $2.95.

Strategic Questions of the Canadian Revolution, edited by Bret Smiley, Vanguard Publications, 1978 (in preparation). $1.95.

Socialism on Trial, by James P. Cannon (includes a debate on defense policy in the Minneapolis Smith Act trial). Pathfinder Press, 1975. 184 pages. $2.95.

COINTELPRO: The FBI's Secret War on Political Freedom, by Nelson Blackstock, with an introduction by Noam Chomsky. Vintage Books, 1976. 216 pages. $3.75.

Watergate and the Myth of American Democracy, by Les Evans and Allen Myers. Pathfinder Press, 1974. 206 pages. $2.95.

FBI vs. Women, by Diane Wang and Cindy Jaquith. Pathfinder Press, 1977. 48 pages. $.75.